Release Your Inner Nerd

Apps, Tech Tools and Tips to Get Organized, Get Creative and Get Ahead

by Beth Ziesenis
Your Nerdy Best Friend

Release Your Inner Nerd:
Apps, Tech Tools and Tips to
Get Organized, Get Creative and Get Ahead

Special discounts are available on quantity purchases by corporations, associations and others. For details, contact the publisher at the address below.

Library of Congress Control Number: 2013912227

ISBN-13: 978-0-615-83836-6 (Your Nerdy Best Friend Ink)
ISBN-10: 0-615-83836-7

Printed in the United States of America

Your Nerdy Best Friend Ink
5694 Mission Center Road, Suite 602-111
San Diego, CA 92108
yournerdybestfriend.com

Dedicated with love to D.J. Rausa,
the most patient and tolerant husband in the world.
I love you even though you'll never read this book
because, as you noted,
it doesn't have a plot.

Special Thanks to the NerdHerd!

In 2012, my original publisher went out of business, so I decided to crowdsource the funding to create this book (see my Kickstarter story, Page 256). Most sincere thanks goes to the many people who joined the NerdHerd and put their faith that this book would become reality.

Thanks to all the NerdHerd members!

AAST Chicago

Alan Wald

Alice Heiman

American Mensa

Amy Hilson

Amy Williams

Anais Lesne

Anne Lupkoski

Barbara Garrett

Barbara Martin

Barbara Murphy

Barbara Rambow

Becky Dryden

Becky Hicks Kinder

Behr Plumbing Service

Beth Bridges

Beth Shumate

Beth Surmont

Brad & Carol Campbell

Bridgette Bienacker

C. Paul Mendez

Cecily Andrews

Charisse Tolano

Chelsea Cameron

Cheryl & Alan Greene

Cheryl & James Sheremeta

Cheryl Paglia

Chris Bowles

Chris Davis

Chris Lyles

Cindy Morgan

Clare Reagan

ConnectCard

Cory Davis

David Blankenship

Dawn Scrofano

Debbi Haddaway

Debbie Lowenthal

Deborah Barnes

Deborah Ragan

Denise Smith

Denise Whitehead

Dennis Carpenter

DeVonne Parks

Release Your Inner Nerd

Diane Mikols	Barcelona	Kathi Cohen
Don Pendley	Janet McEwen	Kathleen Schneider
Dougall McDonald	Jeff Hamstra	Kathleen Wilson
Eileen Behr	Jeff Horn	Kathy Benton
Elizabeth Langston	Jeffrey Wisniewski	Kathy Colabaugh
Elizabeth Shumate	Jennifer Hagen	Kathy Samilo
Emily Arrowsmith	Jennifer Wetherbee	Kelley Drexler
Emily Farrell	Jerry Huffman	Kevin Johnstone
Eric Witmayer	Joan Teeling	Kim Dreher
Eva Lang	Joanne Kim	Kim Williams
Gail Athas	Joanne St-Pierre	Kimberly Lilley
Gary Rifkin	Johanne Stogran	Laura Collins
Gianna Caruso	John Krall	Laura Reed
Gina Sutherland	John Pike	LeAnn Greer
Ginny Fountain	John Tolson	Leigh Ann Senoussi
Harold Bach	Judith Briles	Leigh Faircloth
Harold Goldstein	Judy Kuban	Leslie Herberger
Holly Clubb	Judy Letterman	Leslie White
Holly Clynch	Julia Slocombe	Lightworkers Directory
IAAP VIP Chapter	Julie Mills	
Ian Roxburgh	Julie Schwertfeger	Lillian Mayo
IPWEA	Karen Meyer	Linda Chreno
Jackie Eder-Van Hook	Karen Schneiderman	Linda Fry
	Karen Yoho	Linda Milcos
James Tinsley	Karla Pollack	Linda Weppner
Jamison & Ashton	Katherine Yates	Lisa Farquharson

Release Your Inner Nerd

Lisa Karnes

Lissa Clayborn

Loretta Peskin

Lori Rose

Mackenzie Slayton

Malik Ali

Margaret Maes

Maria Baez

Mark & Sherrie Rosenberger

Mary Gayle Thomas

Mary Pendleton

Matthew Nicholas

Melissa Heeke

Michael Shaw

Michele Huber

Michele Hughes

Michele McGraw

Michelle Herrera

Mike Young

Nancy McCulley

Nell Withers McCauley

Nina Akin

Nora Onishi

Norma Baltodano

Olivia Resch

Patricia Yaya

Patty Laveglia

Paula Lerash

Peggy Wunder Moritz

Pesticide Applicators Assn

Philadelphia Alliance

PromoQuest

Raquel Vargas-Whale

Renita Fonseca

Rick Barnes

Rina Gonzales

Robert Talley

Robert Barnes

Robert Holland

Roberta Nichols

Roberta Scarrow

Robin O. Brown

Ross MacDonald

Ruth Neal

Sandi McKellips

Sandy Raffelson

Sara Miller

Scott & Betty Ziesenis

Shannon Carroll

Sheryl Robinson

Socorro Davis

Stacy Patterson

Stephen Michaele

Steve Siefert

Steven Jones

Susan Soares

Suzanne Dana

Tami Alexander

Terri Schroeder

Terry Murphy

Tesha Hoff

The Book Bin

Therese Long

Thomas Wright

Tim Bower

Tim Wilson

Tina Baldwin

Tina Watson

Tom Pauly

Tommy Smith

Tracy Blithe

Valerie Asbury

Vickie Lester

Table of Contents

Chapter 3

Chapter 4

Chapter 5

Chapter 9

Chapter 10

Chapter 11

Table of Contents

Chapter 15

Chapter 16

Chapter 17

Table of Contents

Before You Dive In

10 Things You Should Know

I know that no one ever reads the intro, but here's my Top Ten List of the most important background you need to know about this book.

1. This book will help you Release Your Inner Nerd.

When Joanie Cunningham called Potsie a nerd on the television show *Happy Days*, it was the ultimate insult. But these days, we have the brilliant *Big Bang Theory* with uber-nerdy main characters, not to mention thousands of Mark Zuckerberg-type technology entrepreneurs making kabillions of dollars nerding for a living.

The tide has turned, Fonzie: nerds are in. Or at least that's what I choose to believe (See #9).

For the first time ever, nerds are sought after and celebrated for their expertise. Nerds in the office are the ones who get things done. Nerds can help you crop a newly indicted ex-employee out of the staff picture. Nerds can show you how to send a large file to your committee members without crashing everyone's email. Nerds can help you find low-cost solutions for virtual meetings. And nerds know the secrets to getting the most out of your new iPad.

With this book, YOU can be the office nerd. Whether you're a first-time iPad owner or a fulltime technology aficionado with a roomful of gadgets, you'll find tech tools and tips to make your life easier, amaze your colleagues, cross tasks off your to-do lists and get things done.

2. The 450+ tools in this book are free or darn cheap.

How many times have you thought to yourself, "Sure, that technology is pricy, but we have an unlimited budget, right?" Chances are you can't afford to pay hundreds of dollars for software or sign up for a pricy subscription for a service—or even if you can afford it, who wants to spend more than she has to? I focus on tech tools that are free or reasonably priced for the services they provide. As such, they're often a basic version of their full-featured technology. Sometimes the tools are free because they're in beta testing and will probably go up in price once they launch. Some tools are free offerings from the open-source community, supported by programmers who volunteer their time to advance technology (or get funding from other sources). Whatever the reason for the low price, we should take advantage of these resources while they're affordable.

3. This book is out of date.

Bummer, huh? You invest in a great book, and the author says the material has changed even before you check anything out! Because technology changes so amazingly fast, you can expect that these tools are going to add features, change pricing, expand to other platforms and be bought out by Google faster than you can turn pages. But... (See #4)

4. This book is constantly updated!

Thanks to the wonders of technology, all you need to do is download Layar (Page 201) to your mobile device and scan this box to get the latest updates and information from Your Nerdy Best Friend!

This book is interactive!
Scan with the Layar App for updates, bonus material and more

5. This book is not a directory.

My first book, *Upgrade to Free: The Best Free and Low-Cost Online Tools and Apps*, came out in 2011, but I sent the first manuscript off to the publisher in April of 2010, one week before Apple announced the first iPad. At the time, the 300+ tools I included were, conservatively, a good representation of everything in the tech universe.

As you probably know, technology has exploded to include approximately a kabillion times the number of tech tools since then. So this time, I concentrated more on categories of technology that can help you at work and home, and I selected a few of the best as samples. For every one of the 450+ tools in this book, I probably reviewed five competitors.

6. I trust these tools as much as I trust any electronic resource.

Are these tools safe, you ask? That's the magic question. Every time I present, people ask if it's safe to store information in the clouds, or if I'm concerned about getting hacked.

I'm confident I did everything I could to verify the safety of the tools I chose to highlight. Many of these I use myself, and I meticulously researched the reputations of the tools that were new to me. But we all assume a certain amount of risk by giving the companies that create these tools access our online data, files, passwords and more.

We should all be concerned about our electronic safety all the time. Nothing is really safe, but here are five ways to guard yourself against the bad guys who offer free tools with hidden agendas:

1. Register with care and use temporary emails until you trust a new resource

2. Keep your virus software up to date

3. Download your free and low-cost software from trusted clearinghouses such as SourceForge and CNET

4. Search the web with the name of a new tool to look for reviews or alerts

5. Go with organizations that will do as much as possible to guard their reputations

7. This book will help fight cancer.

Cancer sucks. There's just no other way to say it. My mother is battling the noxious disease, and too many of my friends and family members have been victims. Cancer research is the key to preventing more pain and suffering, and we want to help. Thus we will donate 10 percent of the profits of the sale of this book to The Leukemia & Lymphoma Society. My husband and I have completed many programs through their endurance athletic division, Team In Training, and we are happy to add contributions from the sale of this book to the thousands we've already raised in pursuit of a cure.

8. Cupcakes are the perfect food.

Throughout the book, you'll find references to my love of cupcakes. To me there is no more perfect balance of sweet and more sweet than a cupcake. And when you lick the frosting off a cupcake, you're left with a muffin… and muffins are healthy, right? (I read that on the internet, so it must be true).

9. I really am a nerd.

I started collecting and sharing tech tools in 2008 after a question about favorite tech tools to a virtual community with the American Society of Association Executives revealed people's rabid interest in the topic. But I've always been fascinated with computers and electronics, starting with my love of Pong, the first home video game. Then came the Commodore 64 computer, DOS commands, WordPerfect templates over the keyboard, my first Macintosh computer in grad school and on and on. Even if I didn't have an audience to share these tools with, I'd still obsess over them. Just ask my husband—I drive him nuts.

10. This book is just a piece of the nerdy universe.

Want more tools? We got 'em! Visit yournerdybestfriend.com for the latest updates and newest tools, and sign up for our newsletter, NerdWords, for a weekly dose of nerdy awesomeness.

Chapter 1

Cloud Computing, Backups and Remote Access

In this chapter:

A computer used to be a box on a desk; and to do computer work, we had to be in front of that box. Now, our files and applications have moved into the cloud, which means that we can be almost anywhere and do almost anything using almost any device. We can also back up the heck out of everything—which, in this dangerous age of hacking, viruses and other nastiness—we should.

Online Backup Solutions

ADrive

AVG LiveKive

Carbonite

CrashPlan

IDrive

Mozy

SOS Online Backup

It's a little tough to talk about pure backup tools these days because the lines are blurred between tools that back stuff up and tools that synchronize tools to all your devices and the cloud.

Me, I'm a cloud-sync girl. I rely on Dropbox (Page 8) to cover my rear if my main computer starts smoking. But the truth is that Dropbox isn't enough to safeguard my data. Dropbox backs up what I have on my computers; and if what I have on my computers is infected with something awful, then everything I own will be infected as well. Of course, Dropbox offers the capability to revert to previous versions, but it really shouldn't be considered a true backup system.

For the online backup services, you generally set up an account; tell them which drives, folders and files to back up; and let them get to work. They can work in the background all the time or back up on a schedule. If your computer blows up, you can restore your files to another machine or recover an earlier version of a document. (Ever hit "Save" instead of "Save As …"?)

2

Chapter 1 ~ Cloud Computing, Backups and Remote Access

If I didn't use Dropbox for my backup plan, I'd choose **CrashPlan.** The free version, aptly named CrashPlan Free, puts the backup network into your hands by allowing you to connect to friends' computers for storage. You back up to someone else's computer while he stores his backup on yours. Neither one of you can see the other's files, but everyone has peace of mind—without a price tag.

Its paid versions are pretty comparable to other services—$59.99/year for unlimited data from one computer. It also offers to save multiple versions of your active files as well as all the files you delete. And you can back up to multiple locations, such as its online cloud, another computer and an external hard drive.

I need to mention **Carbonite** and **Mozy** because they've been around the longest and are perhaps the best-known, but I think these days you have better options. Carbonite looks great on paper—unlimited storage on unlimited devices for $59 a year. But if you read the small print, you'll soon discover that if you have more than 200GB to back up, your backups will be slower and take longer—data throttling, if you will. That said, it's a simple service with a great reputation; so if you don't need 200GB+, it's a nice option.

Mozy was one of the first online backup services I discovered. These days, it also has Mozy Stash, which is its file synchronization service. You can have 2GB for free, or choose a paid plan starting at $5.99/month for up to 50GB.

SOS Online Backup doesn't have a free level, but it's won plenty of awards and high marks. **IDrive** is another standout in this field. It has a fairly generous free plan, and the paid plans start at 150GB for less than $50/year. I love the fact that it integrates with Facebook, which means

3

you can share files and folders with your friends with a couple clicks. IDrive keeps a whopping 30 versions of each file, and it backs up multiple devices into the same account.

IDrive is a good example of the mixing of the pure storage sites and the collaboration/sync cloud services. You can sign up for the classic IDrive storage or go for IDriveSync for a Dropbox-like experience with up to 10GB of storage for free.

ADrive also stands out in the pack because of its free level—a very generous 50GB of storage, which is at least five times the free space of most services. **AVG LiveKive** is a cool option from a trusted company. It has a free 5GB version, as do many of the others; but its unlimited device/unlimited storage version for $79.99/year is an incredible deal. As with Carbonite, though, you should read the fine print, which says that if you have more than 500GB of stuff (which is a LOT of stuff), it might charge you extra.

Social Site Backup Solutions

Backupify

SocialSafe

Are your tweets and Facebook postings works of art? **Backupify** can help you preserve them forever so your kids and grandkids have a permanent record of what you ate for breakfast every day and your reviews of local cupcake shops.

When I first heard about this tool, I thought it was a nutty idea. Why would you need to keep a copy of your Facebook posts? And who wants to keep all the old tweets?

But some high-profile hacks in 2012 brought all kinds of important questions into play. If Facebook fails, what happens to all the awesome photo albums you've created? And how can you get back all your Gmail contacts if the service blows up one day?

Preserving your online data from services such as Gmail (Page 103), Flickr (Page 12), Basecamp (Page 62) and social networks can protect you from hackers, prevent loss of valuable data and perhaps keep you in compliance if you are required to keep records of your online data for legal reasons. When you put it like that, backing up your online stuff makes more sense.

You could also try **SocialSafe,** a newer company with fewer integrations. Instead of backing up your information to the cloud like Backupify does, SocialSafe stores the backups on your own computer. The price difference is major: SocialSafe starts at $6.99/year for up to four services, while you'll pay $4.99/month for up to five with Backupify.

NerdHerd Favorite: Acronis True Image 2013

Jeffrey S. Wisniewski recommends **Acronis True Image 2013**, a Windows program that not only backs up your files but also exact configuration of your PC including your operating system, settings and applications.

Backup Tools at a Glance

(recommended tools in **bold**)

Acronis True Image 2013	Disk imaging and backup system for PCs	$49.99	acronis.com
ADrive	Online backup service with 50GB free	Free for 50GB, or paid plans starting at $6.95/month	adrive.com
AVG LiveKive	Online backup with unlimited storage and unlimited devices for $79.99/year	Free for up to 5GB; or several paid levels, including unlimited devices and unlimited storage for $79.99/year	avg.com/us-en/ avg-livekive
Backupify	**Backup solution for online data such as Gmail, Facebook, Twitter, Basecamp and Flickr**	**Free up to 3 services and 1GB, or paid plans start at $4.99/month for 10GB and 5 services**	**backupify.com**
Carbonite	Online backup system with (limited) unlimited storage	Unlimited storage starts at $59/year	carbonite.com
CrashPlan	**Free backup system for peer-to-peer connections, plus paid plans and mobile apps**	**Free for buddy backup connections, or starting at $32.99/month for paid plans**	**crashplan.com**
IDrive	Online backup service with 5GB free and multiple device backup	Free for 5GB, or starting at $49.50/year for 150GB	idrive.com
Mozy	Online backup system with 2GB free, file synching (beta) and mobile apps	Free for up to 2GB, or starting at $5.99/month for 50GB	mozy.com
SocialSafe	Social media backup service with local storage instead of online backups	Starting at $6.99/year for up to 4 services	socialsafe.net
SOS Online Backup	Online backup for computers and devices	Starting at $99.99/year for 5 devices	sosonlinebackup.com

Cloud Synchronization Tools

If I had to pick one category of technological breakthroughs that has transformed the way I do business, it would have to be the services that allow you to have your hard drive in the sky. That means that anything you store in a cloud-based, file-sync site will be available to you anywhere you have access to a smart device or computer.

Let's say you have a critical sales meeting across the country. In the old days, you might work on the slide deck on your desktop computer and save it to a thumb drive or, even further back, to a floppy disk—the 5.25-inch disks that were actually floppy! Then you'd bring your precious PowerPoint to your laptop to work on the plane and either save it back to the portable drive or the laptop. When you arrive at your sales meeting, you might have to load your presentation into another machine; and, in no time at all, your presentation has multiple versions on multiple computers, and you're left with a mystery as to which file you need to convince your clients to hire you. And if your boss gets his hands in the mix and makes changes, the confusion increases by a magnitude of 10. Maddening!

Cloud-based file synchronization erases all the hassle. You simply place all your important files into designated folders; and those folders are instantly updated everywhere you have the software installed, plus it's available directly from the service's site. You can share your folder with your boss, who can make all the changes he wants. And then you have the power to go back to your favorite version if he messed it all up.

When you store your files in the cloud in a synchronized system, they are available any time you need them, even if you spill your hot tea on your laptop on the plane and the machine starts smoking.

Because these tools are so popular, the competition in this category is fierce, with shiny, new services launching all the time. Thus, it's a challenge to identify the top tools; but I'm sticking with the top five that have been around the longest, have the most integrations and appear most often in other top lists. But before the top five, here's an in-depth view of my favorite.

Dropbox

I could not, would not, cannot live without Dropbox.

Well, perhaps I'm exaggerating a tad. I could probably survive without a robust cloud synchronization service like Dropbox, but I sure wouldn't want to. Dropbox is my favorite probably because I've been using it so long that everything is all set up. It's also arguably the biggest and most established service in this category.

Dropbox has changed the way I work in so many ways, especially because of the myriad third-party services.

Here are three of the many ways Dropbox makes my life easier.

Reason 1: Easy Hard-Drive Transfers

When I retired my old PC desktop and replaced it with my shiny new MacBook Air, I put off switching computers because I dreaded moving all the stuff from the old computer to the new one. Instead of trying to network the two computers to transfer stuff from one hard drive to the other, I simply put everything on my PC into my Dropbox and made sure the MacBook Air was connected to the Internet.

It took several hours, but now every file I have is stored on Dropbox's site as well as my new laptop. Yes, I had to upgrade to a paid version, but it was worth it.

Reason 2: Oops Proof

I hired a guy to download logos for the tools I'm using in this book. We shared a Dropbox folder; and when the project was finished, I didn't do anything with the folder for a couple of weeks.

When I went to get the logos, GARG! The folder was GONE! The guy had deleted our shared folder after the project was done. I simultaneously felt sick to my stomach and hot under the collar, but then I remembered that Dropbox lets me restore deleted files (for up to 30 days on my plan) and revert to older versions. Problem averted before I even had to reach for the Alka-Seltzer.

Reason 3: Collaboration Super Station

When my husband and I bought our house, our financial guy needed every single financial document ever produced. (I think he even asked for a profit/loss statement from my second-grade lemonade stand.) I simply created and shared a Dropbox folder with my husband and the financial guy.

My husband and I moved the documents the finance guy needed to the folder, and he instantly had them on his desktop. We all knew what documents we had at a glance, and we never played the "email, email—who's got the email?" game with attachments.

NerdHerd Thumbs Up: Dropbox

Dropbox is beloved by NerdHerders as well! "It changed my life," says Vickie Lester. Amy Hilson says it's great for personal and business use and super easy to use. Alan Wald from International Association of Plumbing and Mechanical Officials loves it because he says, "I know I can avoid emailing files back and forth between computers, smartphones and tablets. And Leslie Herberger counts it as one of her favorites (See her top shopping tools, Page 133).

Common Characteristics

Most of the major players in this field have many of the same characteristics and capabilities as Dropbox. Here's a summary of the features you'll find in most (if not all) of the top tools.

✔ Free storage of 2-10GB, with the capability to earn more when you spread the word

✔ Web and mobile apps to access your files from anywhere

✔ Real-time synchronization wherever the service is installed

✔ Capability to restore deleted files and older versions

✔ Collaboration via shared folders or files (Some services have different levels of permissions for shared items.)

✔ Instant file and folder sharing via links, no matter the size

✔ Integration with third-party apps for enhanced features and accessibility

Top Five Cloud Synchronization Apps (recommended tools in **bold**)

Name	Free Storage	Starting Paid Versions	Super Power	Kryptonite
Dropbox	**2GB**	**$9.99/month for up to 100GB**	• **Well established** • **Lots of third-party integrations** • **High profile**	• **On the pricy side** • **No permission settings for shared folders**
Box	5GB	$15/user/month for up to 1,000GB	• Lots of third-party integrations • Well established • Earn up to 50GB free storage	• No full-text search in free versions • No version history
Google Drive	5GB	$2.49/month for up to 25GB	• Ummm—it's Google! • Create and edit Drive files in Google Docs	• Storage is shared with photos from Picasa • Google Docs default editing can be annoying
Microsoft SkyDrive	7GB	$10/year for 20GB	• Smooth integration with Microsoft products • Darn cheap • Create and edit documents with Office Web Apps • Cool "Fetch" feature lets you retrieve PC files even if they're not in sync folder	• Runs on Microsoft Silverlight, which is sometimes flaky • May limit the number of files you can update per month • Doesn't play as well with Macs
SugarSync	5GB	$49.99/year for 30GB	• Sync any folder on your computer, not just the SugarSync folder • Permission levels for shared files and folders	• It seems to have a problem synchronizing QuickBooks files

Online Photo Storage

Flickr

Photobucket

Picasa

Shutterfly

SmugMug

You can always use cloud storage sites to organize and back up your photos, but there are several services that specialize in image files; and they are designed to help you organize, share and edit photos inside the tool.

Let's start with an online photo storage tool that's not actually designed for photo storage. **Picasa** is a super-secret weapon for getting your graphic library into shape. Install this free program (courtesy of Google), and it searches your entire computer for all graphic files. The program leaves the files where they are, but the Picasa interface now gives you access to see everything.

In just a few minutes, you can find duplicate picture files, add names to pictures (especially easy if you sign in to Google and use your Gmail contacts) and create folders. You can also create folders and files to share with others and store them in your Google Drive account (5GB free).

But one of the most awesome tools is hidden under the hood—editing with my favorite tools from the long-lost Picnik web app! Google purchased it a few years ago, much to my dismay. But now the easy editing tools are available in Picasa, along with easy collage-making capabilities.

Flickr is a grandfather in the cloud-storage department, invented way before we ever started using the word "cloud."

Owned by Yahoo!, Flickr in and of itself is pretty simple. You upload photos, and there you have them: uploaded photos. You can organize them into albums, tag them or share them with friends. But one of the coolest things about Flickr these days is its "App Garden," which holds approximately 1TB of third-party apps that integrate with your Flickr feed.

12

The apps allow you to do everything from back up your Flickr collection to automatically upload and organize. Plus, there are any number of tools to edit your photos.

Photobucket is another cloud storage solution for pictures, allowing up to 2GB free. As with other services, you can share photos or keep them private. Photobucket uses Aviary photo editing tools to add borders, crop and add filters.

My sister uses **Shutterfly** to share the adorable photos of my adorable nephews, with the peace of mind that Shutterfly defaults all the uploads to private and specializes in sharing personal photos with small groups, such as classrooms, sports teams and families.

Shutterfly makes its money by encouraging you to buy prints and gifts from your photos and makes it ridiculously easy to do so. That's why our favorite gift from my sister is the annual family calendar, with photos of all of us with the kids throughout the year, along with birthdays and important family dates.

Because Shutterfly wants you to buy stuff to pay for its services, it won't let you download a high-res version of your upload. If you want the full-resolution photos, you're going to have to pay $10 or more plus shipping and handling for an archive DVD.

Oh, and surprise! Looks like Shutterfly partnered with my favorite multi-media video maker Animoto (Page 170) so you can create "Videograms" from your Shutterfly pictures for $30/year (the same price as a subscription to Animoto).

Finally, if you're really good at taking pictures, I'm talking coffee-shop gallery good, you might consider **SmugMug,** a photo storage and sharing site made for amateur and professional photographers. The site can be a beautiful backdrop for your photo portfolio, and the higher subscription levels even integrate with e-commerce options to sell your masterpieces. SmugMug is quite reasonably priced: unlimited photos starting at $40/year.

NerdHerd Thumbs Up: Shutterfly and Picasa

Roki Vargas, who happens to be my best friend from college, uses Shutterfly to create books full of memories for her mother and grandmother. Linda Weppner from Century 21 Bell Real Estate says of Picasa, "I finally have all of my pictures in one place!"

Online Photo Storage at a Glance
(recommended tools in **bold**)

Flickr	Online photo storage and sharing	Free for up to 300MB of uploads a month, with only the most recent 200 photos available in the stream, or unlimited subscription levels starting at $1.87/month for 2-year commitment	flickr.com
Photobucket	Online and desktop photo storage service that imports your Facebook photos with a click	Free for up to 2GB, or paid plans start at $29.99/year or 20GB	photobucket.com
Picasa	**Photo organizing, editing and sharing software**	**Free for desktop app and up to 5GB free storage online with Google Drive**	**picasa.google.com**
Shutterfly	**Online photo storage and sharing with family-friendly protection**	**Free for unlimited photo storage**	**shutterfly.com**
SmugMug	Online photo storage service for avid photographers	Unlimited storage starting at $40/year	smugmug.com

Chapter 2

Computer Tools and Utilities

We've all seen plenty of scary statistics about computer security, yet I'm sorry to say that few of us do everything we can to protect our personal devices or our online browsing. I've jumped up and down and waggled my finger until I can waggle no more, trying to get people to be more aware of today's dangers.

Although nothing is 100 percent foolproof against hackers and viruses these days (I mean, if eHarmony isn't safe, nothing is, right?), we all have access to a host of free and bargain tools that will do their best to keep malware, viruses and other nasties from taking over our computers and our lives. Plus, you can find bunches of other helpful tech tools for your computer for little or no cost.

Computer Security Tools

avast!

AVG Free

CCleaner

iAntivirus

Malwarebytes

Spybot—Search and Destroy

WinPatrol

New computers often come with a trial version of a major computer security suite such as Norton or McAfee, and with good reason. In 2012, McAfee released a study that says 1-in-6 PCs is unprotected. I've seen studies that show that an unprotected PC will be probed for vulnerabilities within hours—maybe even minutes—of connecting to the Internet. Yipes!

The people who write the warning pop-ups for the built-in security programs should get Pulitzers because they are incredibly effective. Who can resist a note like this?

"STOP! If you don't install our full version of this software, your computer will be unprotected and will soon be seething with horrible worms and Trojans!"

Most of the time, I jump right into the program's shopping cart and rush to protect my computer for just $49.99 for a year's worth of security. But the truth is that we don't have to pay a ton of money to protect our investments.

AVG Free and **avast!** are usually at the top of the lists of free computer security tools, although they both have moderately priced full versions that are worth the expense. **Spybot—Search and Destroy's** free version is completely awesome and unobtrusive and can run side-by-side with your regular antivirus software. Spybot's main function is to find and get rid of sneaky programs that often install themselves when you click advertisements or install free software with annoying or dangerous add-ons.

WinPatrol is another good security device that can run alongside your regular security systems, and **CCleaner** keeps files and systems tidy. And if you do find yourself in trouble with a bug you can't get rid of, **Malwarebytes** is excellent for removing all traces of an active threat.

You may have noticed that most of these tools are for PCs, not Macs. Macs for the most part have been isolated from most security threats, although their rising popularity means rising problems. The newest Mac operating systems have some pretty hefty controls when it comes to downloads, meaning nothing can be installed without permission (or that's the way it's supposed to work). Just in case, I use **iAntivirus**, a free app from Norton, to scan my MacBook Air.

This book is interactive!
Scan with the Layar App for
updates, bonus material and more

Computer Security Tools at a Glance (recommended tools in **bold**)

avast!	Free antivirus software for PC and Mac	Free for standard software, more features in Pro versions for yearly fees (prices vary)	avast.com
AVG Free	**Windows-based anti-virus and spyware software**	**Free for AVG Free; paid versions with extra features start at $35.99**	**free.avg.com**
CCleaner	Easy-to-use computer cleaner for PC or Mac	Free	piriform.com/ ccleaner
iAntivirus	**Free antivirus app for Mac**	**Free**	**iantivirus.com**
Malwarebytes	Malware and threat detection and removal tool	Free for standard tool, or auto-updating, faster version for $24.95	malwarebytes.org
Spybot— Search and Destroy	**Adware, malware and spyware scanner for Windows**	**Free for personal use; paid versions start at $13.99/year**	**safer- networking.org**
WinPatrol	Windows-based PC cleaner and monitor	Free for basic features, $30 for lifetime license	winpatrol.com

IT Tools

My eyes kind of cross when I start reading about registry keys or defragging a computer or root booting or whatever they call it. I may be an app queen, but I can't take a computer apart and put it back together; and I really don't have much of an idea how computers actually work. But I do know where to find a few awesome tools and resources to keep your system and programs updated and running smoothly.

Download Managers

Allmyapps

FileHippo

Ninite

When I switched to Mac in 2012, I discovered the beautiful App Store, where all the programs I could ever want or need are neatly organized in a marketplace and automatically updated and installed. **Allmyapps** is a seriously cool Windows resource that pretty much does the same thing. It gives you the option of choosing apps and software to install with a few clicks of your mouse, avoiding hours of work, especially when you're setting up a new computer. Plus, your downloads can be synced across all your PCs, so you will always have the same programs available.

I can put together a list of essential apps for employees of Your Nerdy Best Friend, such as Dropbox (Page 8), LastPass (Page 21) and LogMeIn (Page 70). That way, the new folks will just have to download the Allmyapps software and use my list to be able to have all the tools we use from Day 1.

Ninite is similar to Allmyapps—it's not as fancy, nor does it offer the extensive list that Allmyapps does. But it's a sentimental favorite in my book since I discovered it years ago and saying the name brings back memories of childhood (as in, "Ni-nite, Mommy.").

FileHippo has also been around for a while. This handy site and downloadable tool helps Windows users discover when to update freeware programs.

Technical Support

GeekBuddy

Twelpforce

Ever take an IT guy to lunch to get him to look at your computer? It's so annoying when something on your machine is broken and you don't have the time, resources or knowledge to figure it out.

My first step when I have a computer mystery is to send a tweet on Twitter to **Twelpforce.** (Say that three times fast.) OK, actually my first steps are to curse, grit my teeth and reach for a stress-relieving cupcake. Then I tweet. Twelpforce is an ingenious idea from Best Buy. The management team empowers all the Best Buy employees to share their technical knowledge for free with anyone who asks for help. I became a believer soon after I bought my first iPhone. I was frustrated for weeks because I could receive mail but not send it. Believe it or not, yelling at the dang phone didn't do any good, nor did any of the button mashing or cussing.

With much skepticism, I tweeted my problem to @Twelpforce; and within three minutes, an employee was asking me questions. Five minutes after that, he sent me a link to a video on my own email provider's site with clear instructions to enable sending.

Another geek repository with a great reputation is **GeekBuddy,** a service of Comodo, a well-respected computer security/antivirus company. A mere $5/month sounds like a good investment to have a computer expert at your command. The technician can help with a variety of everyday computer challenges, from setting up your email to taking over your computer to help you get rid of a virus.

IT Tools at a Glance

(recommended tools in **bold**)

Allmyapps	Windows download manager that resembles the Apple App Store	Free	allmyapps.com
FileHippo.com	Tool to quickly discover and update PC software	Free	filehippo.com
GeekBuddy	Instant tech help for PCs	$4.95/month, less for longer subscriptions	geekbuddy.com
Ninite	Windows download manager to install or update multiple programs at once	Free for personal use, or $20/month for professional	ninite.com
Twelpforce	**Twitter-based tech help from the friendly technology experts at Best Buy**	**Free**	**twitter.com/ twelpforce**

Disposable Email Addresses

Dead Address

Guerrilla Mail

Mailinator

Melt Mail

spamgourmet

I hate to admit it, but even I've been duped into registering with a company that sells my email address. That's why I love services like **Mailinator,** which gives you a temporary email address to use for your registration.

Mailinator lets you create new inboxes on the fly, just by putting a keyword in front of @mailinator.com (or any of its hundreds of domains).

You can also go to sites such as **Guerrilla Mail, Dead Address, spamgourmet** and **Melt Mail** for an address, use it to register for something, then return to the sites if you need to click on an additional link to complete the registration. Depending on the service you use, your email will be good for a few minutes or a little longer if you need it.

Password Managers

KeePass

LastPass

PasswordCard

RoboForm

YubiKey

OK, it's time to have a serious conversation about your computer security. When 6.5 million passwords were hacked at LinkedIn, we all had a wake-up call about our passwords and web habits. One of the most common mistakes we make, besides picking passwords that are too easy, is that we use the same password for multiple sites. And if a bad guy has our username and password from one site, he could try the password out on other sites and eventually get to some pretty valuable information.

It's time to truly take charge of your password and Internet security issues. **LastPass** is a free, cloud-based tool that allows you to create one master password to gain access to all your sites. Further, I love that as soon as you install it, it scrapes all the sites in your browser history to show you just how many you have and how insecure you really are.

It's a little disconcerting to put everything in LastPass' hands, but CNET, PCWorld and Lifehacker all give it a thumbs up. **RoboForm** and **KeePass** also get high marks, but I can't bring myself to use KeePass because it seems to be one "p" short of a socially acceptable name. (I keep reading it as "Keep-ass.")

The next step up from sticky notes is an innovative little site called **PasswordCard.** You generate a unique and complicated wallet-sized card that helps you choose random passwords for all your sites. PasswordCard also has an app to let you carry your card with you electronically. For $25, you could also purchase a **YubiKey.** Just push a button on this little USB device, and it'll insert a crazy-complicated password into any new password field. Then the next time you visit that site, you simply insert your YubiKey into the port, and your password appears. This sounds like an awesome solution for people who can keep track of all their little gadgets, but I know I'd lose the dang thing right away.

For the ultimate password security, stay tuned. A team at UC Berkeley's School of Information is working on wearable technology that will read your brainwaves so you can think your password to get into a site. Creepy or awesome? I think it's both, but I'd probably give it a try.

NerdHerd Thumbs Up: Roboform

Joanne St-Pierre from Niagara Falls Tourism loves that Roboform remembers her passwords. "It's a great tool for people over the age of 50!"

Security Alert: Online Security Tools

If you don't get anything else from this book, please take this part seriously: It's time to really take a good look at your password habits and online security.

People in my sessions ask me all the time— are these tech tools safe? And my pessimistic answer is—probably not, because *nothing* is safe these days.

When I say nothing, I mean it. The high-profile security breaches in 2012 were mind-boggling: Dropbox, Zappos, eHarmony, Yahoo, the state of South Carolina. No online system is immune from bad people who want to steal information to do bad things, not to mention the goofballs who hack into stuff just to show that we're vulnerable. But we nerds are willing to accept these risks to reap the many benefits of today's technology, although we must do whatever we can to limit our exposure.

Online Security Tools at a Glance
(recommended tools in **bold**)

Dead Address	Disposable email service with no time limit	Free	deadaddress.com
Guerrilla Mail	60-minute disposable email service	Free	guerrillamail.com
How Secure Is My Password	**Password security checker**	**Free**	**howsecureismypassword.net**
KeePass	Free, open-source password manager	Free	keepass.info

Online Security Tools at a Glance (continued)

LastPass	Password manager with mobile apps	Free for basic, or $12/ year for full version	lastpass.com
Mailinator	Disposable email service with on-the-fly inbox creation	Free	mailinator.com
Melt Mail	Disposable email service (up to 24 hours)	Free	meltmail.com
PasswordCard	Printable and app-based password manager	Free	passwordcard.org
RoboForm	Form-filler and password manager	Starts at $9.95/year	roboform.com
spamgourmet	Disguised email service with advanced features	Free	spamgourmet.com
YubiKey	USB device for password management	$25	yubico.com

Behind the Glasses: Password Confessions

When I installed LastPass and did the initial sweep of my browser history, I almost turned in my NerdCard. I was registered on 121 sites, and 81 of those had *the same password*. What's more, this password was one I had been using since at least 2005, the six-letter name of a family member. Bad, bad nerd! During the next several months, I worked through the entire list of registrations and replaced the ridiculously easy password with LastPass-generated ones that, according to **howsecureismypassword.net,** would take password-hacking software more than a year to figure out.

Chapter 3

• •

Essential Office Software

Every office needs certain software and resources to function, essential tools such as word processors, spreadsheet software, a way to work with PDFs. In the old days (maybe five years ago?), we all relied on Microsoft for the majority of our "office suites"; but the startup price for the business-level packages can be quite steep.

These days, you have a number of low-cost and even free alternatives to these expensive essentials; and most of them have evolved to the point that they are compatible with equivalent programs.

Office Suites

Apache OpenOffice

Google Docs

iWork

LibreOffice

Office Web Apps

Zoho

One of the pioneers into the Office-knockoff market was **Apache OpenOffice,** released in 2002. Somewhere along the way, a branch broke off; and **LibreOffice** was born. The two downloadable suites, now competitors, are both well-known free options to Microsoft Office; and both offer comparable word processing, spreadsheet, presentation, drawing and database tools. Rumor has it that LibreOffice is making great strides as a serious contender to Microsoft products.

Other office suites offer free productivity in the cloud. **Google Docs** is great for sharing documents, online collaboration and anywhere access, although the features of the program are on the basic side, at least for a heavy Microsoft Office user like myself. **Zoho** has similar cloud-based office software for word processing, spreadsheets, note organization and presentations. If you're on a Mac, you'll definitely want to check out Apple's **iWork** suite, which includes Pages for word processing, Numbers for spreadsheets and Keynote for presentations (Page 195). I didn't find that this $60 replacement ($19.99/program) did everything I wanted (See Behind the Glasses: Your Nerdy Best Friend's Essential Software, Page 30), but it has strong features for about half the price of Microsoft's Mac suite.

Microsoft offers its own free suite, **Office Web Apps,** with lite versions of Word, Excel, PowerPoint and OneNote, as well as the separate email site, Outlook.com.

Mobile Office Apps

Documents To Go

iWork Apps

Office Mobile

Quickoffice

When it comes to accessing and editing your office documents on the go, you have several options, but I frankly find them inconvenient to use. I don't like writing and reviewing documents on the smaller mobile screens, and don't even get me started on trying to touch the right cell to edit a spreadsheet.

Logic would dictate that Microsoft's **Office Mobile** would be the best app to access Microsoft documents, but the early versions don't seem to be the perfect answer. The first challenge is that it's only available to people who subscribe to Office 365. Secondly, first reviewers report pretty basic functionality on par with the somewhat limited Office Web Apps. And finally, the app is not yet available for iPad or any Android devices, although all the programs are already installed on all Windows Phones.

My favorite mobile office suite (probably because I downloaded it first) is **Documents To Go**, a veteran in this area, which is available on a number of mobile platforms. My second favorite is **Quickoffice** for Android and iOS. Quickoffice might be the app to watch because rumor has it that its new owner, Google, has big plans for a Microsoft online suite competition. Both let you access your files from other cloud services and sync and share to your heart's content. If I used the iWork Suite (Page 26) on my Mac, I'd love the comparable **iWork apps**. In my opinion, these apps most closely mimic the desktop/laptop editing experience.

NerdHerd Thumbs Up: CloudOn

NerdHerder Kim W. from The Corydon Group gives **CloudOn** a pat on the back. CloudOn offers the same types of editing, access and collaboration features as the other mobile office suites for free!

Office Suites at a Glance
(recommended tools in **bold**)

Apache OpenOffice	Downloadable open-source office software suite for word processing, spreadsheets, presentations, graphics and databases	Free	openoffice.org
CloudOn	Mobile office app for iOS and Android	Free	cloudon.com
Documents To Go	**Mobile office suite app for iOS, BlackBerry and more**	**Varies from free to $19.99**	**dataviz.com/ dtg_home.html**
Google Docs	**Free online office suite with word processing, spreadsheets, forms, presentations and a drawing app**	**Free**	**docs.google.com**

Office Suites at a Glance (continued)

iWork	Apple office suite for Mac and iOS devices	$9.99/app for iOS devices; $19.99/ program for Mac	apple.com/iwork
LibreOffice	**Downloadable open-source office software suite for word processing, spreadsheets, presentations, graphics and databases**	**Free**	**libreoffice.org**
Office Mobile	Microsoft office suite of products for iPhone	Free for Office365 subscribers	office.microsoft.com/ mobile
Office Web Apps	Online modified office suite from Microsoft with Word, Excel, OneNote and PowerPoint	Free for Office Web Apps, and Office365 has full versions for $99.99/year for up to 5 machines	office.microsoft.com/ web-apps
Quickoffice	Google's mobile office apps for iOS and Android	$14.99-$19.99	quickoffice.com
Zoho	Online office suite	Free for one user, or group platforms starting at $3/ month/user	zoho.com

Behind the Glasses:
Your Nerdy Best Friend's Essential Software

Whenever I can, I try to practice what I preach by relying on the free and bargain tech tools that I share. When I made the switch to Mac in early 2012, I decided to stop my addiction to Microsoft Office suites and try out the lower-cost options.

My first stop was Google Docs, which I consider to be one of the most hearty office packages around. But I had gotten used to the Microsoft bells and whistles, especially when it came to Word docs. Google Docs is a fairly plain jane program, and it just couldn't compete. Gmail, however, was a pretty good alternative to Outlook, though I was sad to give up my favorite email wrangler, Xobni (see Page 100).

Next I tried Apple's iWork suite for about $60, including Pages for word processing, Numbers for spreadsheets and Keynote for presentations. Keynote was amazing, with completely cool animations and features; but again I was disappointed with Pages, which is the functionality I need the most.

I am embarrassed to admit that I finally gave up and purchased Microsoft Office for Mac with PowerPoint, Word, Excel and Outlook for about $150. But I'm happy to report that I'm finally satisfied. I use Keynote instead of PowerPoint, but Word is just as cool as I remember.

Fax Tools

eFax Free

FaxBetter

FaxOrama

FaxZero

GotFreeFax

It seems strange that in this digital age we still have to deal with paper faxes, but they still have a place in our world. We fax contracts, registration forms and advertisements when email alone won't work and scanning and then emailing would take too long.

I was so happy when I discovered **FaxZero.** What a cool thing. You upload a document or PDF to fax to anyone for free (maximum three pages, two free faxes a day). The cover page will contain an ad—not a problem for most faxes I need to send. But if I need something more professional, I can pay $1.99 and fax up to 15 pages with an ad-free cover sheet. With FaxZero, you can send a fax for free to any fax machine in the United States or Canada, or internationally for a small one-time charge.

FaxOrama is similar but also offers an iOS app for faxing on the go, and **GotFreeFax** leaves out the ad. I know what you're thinking—"Why does Beth use FaxZero when the others sound like better deals?" Because it has a "Z" in it, of course.

A couple of services will also give you numbers to receive faxes, such as **eFax Free** and **FaxBetter,** although they both will charge you for outgoing faxes. eFax Free gives a toll number that you can give out, and your faxes come via email as attachments. You have to download its software to be able to read the attachment, of course; but it's a small price to pay if you don't want to buy an actual fax machine (or figure out how to hook up your all-in-one, which has been sitting in a box in your garage for two years.)

FaxBetter gives you a toll-free number and up to 20 free incoming pages a month, but if you don't get a fax every week, it deactivates your number.

Call Management System

Google Voice	**Google Voice** is in a category of its own. Have you ever had to write an email to someone that says, "If it's after 5 p.m., call on this line; or call the office during the weekdays, unless it's Tuesday, when you can reach me

at the volunteer center"?

Google Voice simplifies your incoming and outgoing calls, and does much more. It's not a phone service; let's call it an advanced call-management system. Most of the awesome features are free, and it can centralize (and revolutionize) your phone and text communications.

Here's a partial list of Google Voice awesomeness:

✔ Custom vanity phone numbers

✔ One number that can route to all your phones

✔ Free and low-cost national and international calls

✔ Free text messaging

✔ Call screening and blocking

✔ Transcribed voicemails

✔ Personalized greetings for different incoming numbers

✔ Conference calls

✔ Call recording and archiving

✔ Mobile apps for multiple operating systems

Phone and Fax Tools at a Glance

(recommended tools in **bold**)

eFax Free	Free outgoing fax number	Free for up to 10 pages per month; plus level starts at $14.13/month	efax.com/ efax-free
FaxBetter	Free toll-free fax number for up to 20 pages/month	Free for up to 20 pages/month, or starting at $5.95/month	faxbetter.com
FaxOrama	Free outgoing fax service with iOS app	Free, up to 2 per day with 5 pages each	faxorama.com
FaxZero	**Free outgoing faxes with ad on cover page**	**Free up to 5 per day, 3 pages each**	**faxzero.com**
Google Voice	**Phone service to organize and manage incoming calls**	**Free to receive number and most features, or transfer mobile number for $20**	**google.com/voice**
GotFreeFax	Ad-free free fax service	Free for up to 2 per day, 3 pages each	gotfreefax.com

File Converters and Openers

File Viewer

FileInfo

Free Opener

Zamzar

Let's say you're working with an incredible graphic designer; and he sends you the first draft of the incredibly important graphic you've commissioned — a graphic you have to unveil at a meeting you're having in three minutes.

You click on this file, knowing you're about to see a masterpiece; and then a frustrating pop-up announces, "Windows cannot open this file. What do you want to do?"

What do I want to do? I want to click on the dang file and have it open, for goodness' sake!

After that message, you either have to write back to your designer to ask for a different format or start running around the Internet to try to find a fix.

Luckily, the World Wide Web has instant fixes for your challenges. This section details both downloadable and online tools that can solve your roadblock in time to get to your meeting with the file you need in formats you can share.

Don't waste a moment of your precious time trying to fight with a file that won't open. Free downloadable software such as **File Viewer** for Mac or **Free Opener** for Windows will allow you to instantly peek into dozens of file types without having to hunt for specialty software or download a new program.

And **Zamzar** is even more handy. This file conversion tool has saved my hide multiple times. Simply visit the site, upload a file, choose what you want to turn it into and press a button. In a matter of minutes, your file is transformed into the format you need.

Wait, there's more! You can convert files via email as well, just by writing to [format]@zamzar.com. For example, you can send your Microsoft Word file to pdf@zamzar.com; and in a few minutes, you'll receive a link to your new pdf. Or you can send your PDF to doc@zamzar.com, and the opposite happens. It's magic either way.

When extensions look suspicious, I head over to **FileInfo** to check them out before clicking. The site is kept up to date with every possible file extension. You can search by file type (audio, game, executables, etc.)

or simply enter the extension into the search engine. Once you know what you're dealing with, the site gives you a list of applications that will open it.

OCR (Optical Character Recognition)

Evernote

FreeOCR

Google Drive

NewOCR

OCR tools solve a challenge I've had multiple times: I receive a PDF that I need to edit in Word or a graphic of text that I need to tweak. Retyping takes too long, and cutting and pasting from a PDF can be frustrating and time-consuming.

On both the **FreeOCR** and **NewOCR** sites, you can upload PDFs, JPEGs or other types of image files; and the sites convert them instantly into editable, searchable text.

The results are usually not quite perfect but darn close. NewOCR also helps you preserve the formatting and page layout so your tables, images, captions and headers don't go haywire in the new document.

Another cool thing: The sites can recognize and process multiple languages.

Google Drive and **Evernote** also have some cool OCR properties. When you upload a PDF into Google Drive, you can choose to pull out the text. And with Evernote, your image files are automatically scanned for text, which is then searchable. If you pay for the full version of Evernote ($45/year), it'll also index the text of any PDF upload.

File Utilities at a Glance

(recommended tools in **bold**)

Evernote	Note-taking tool that scans image and PDF files for search results	Free for image file scans, $45/year for PDFs	evernote.com
File Viewer	Mac download that lets you view any file	Free	macfileviewer.com
FileInfo	**Extensive file-extension list online**	**Free**	**fileinfo.com**
Free Opener	Windows download to open dozens of file types	Free	freeopener.com
FreeOCR	Online OCR service for images and PDFs (first page only)	Free	free-ocr.com
Google Drive	Instant OCR for uploaded PDFs	Free	drive.google.com
NewOCR	**Online OCR service with layout analysis options**	**Free**	**newocr.com**
Zamzar	Convert any file to any format	Free for up to 100MB. Ad-free levels for larger files start at $7/month.	zamzar.com

PDF Tools

Holy moly but has this category taken off! There are now a kabillion (approximately) different free and bargain sites, software packages and apps that compete directly with Adobe. Adobe developed the Portable Document Format (PDF) in the early 1990s as a common document format that would allow fonts, pictures, formatting and styles to be locked into any type of file so that every recipient would see it the same way.

Although Adobe holds patents on the format, PDF has become an open standard; and many competitors provide alternatives to Adobe's fairly pricy software package to create, annotate, merge, alter and fully manipulate the files.

I'm not even going to attempt to give a full list of PDF tools. You can find them as cloud-based sites, stand-alone downloads, browser plug-ins and mobile-device apps. But here are a few major players I use and respect.

Downloadable PDF Tools

Adobe Reader XI

Nitro Reader

PDF Converter Free

PDF Toolkit +

Adobe Reader is on this list? I just spent the previous couple of paragraphs saying how Adobe software was no longer needed because of free and bargain tools and apps. What's up with that, Beth?

If you haven't taken a close look at your regular old Adobe Reader (or you keep avoiding the updates), you are missing out in a big way. Reader XI, released in the fall of 2012, contains capabilities that can change the way you work with PDFs. You can now add notes to documents, cross out and replace text, fill out forms, apply your own signature with a click, and track changes from multiple editors. You can even send up to five documents a month out for signature, complete with tracking, notifications and other fancy features.

I may be jumping to conclusions here, but I believe Adobe added these rich features because the competition has become so aggressive. It had to offer more goodies so we wouldn't go looking for other readers and services.

The Windows-based **Nitro Reader** is a robust free tool as well, with the annotation and signing tools of Adobe Reader XI, as well as the capability to create PDFs, extract images and text, and add security features.

On my Mac, I use Adobe Reader for the annotation and signing, plus two apps from the App Store. **PDF Converter Free** from Wondershare lets me drop a PDF into the dialog box and convert it to a PowerPoint file. **PDF Toolkit** + lets me concatenate and merge PDFs, plus extract pages, images and text.

Online and Mobile PDF Tools

EasypDF Cloud

iAnnotate

PDF Expert

PDF Reader Pro

One of the most exciting developments in the PDF world is the move to mobile PDF tools. Now you can open a PDF on your tablet, sign it with your finger and send it off in minutes.

With tools such as **iAnnotate, PDF Reader Pro** and **PDF Expert,** the days of printing out a document, signing it and faxing it back are ending. What's more, you can mark up a PDF, fill out forms and send to others for comment. And most of the apps in this category will cost you less than a cup of highfalutin' coffee.

Easypdf Cloud lets you drag and drop files into cute little boxes on a super clean site. You can convert files into PDFs or convert PDFs into Word docs. In addition, you can combine different files into one PDF. If you register for a free account, you can hook your Dropbox to the system and batch-convert files.

PDF Tools at a Glance

(recommended tools in **bold**)

Adobe Reader	**Free global standard for reliably viewing, printing, and commenting on PDF documents**	**Free**	**adobe.com products/reader**
easyPDF Cloud	**Online tool to convert files to PDF, convert PDFs to Word and merge PDFs**	**Free, no registration needed; but registration adds features such as batch batch conversions**	**easypdfcloud.com**
iAnnotate	PDF tool for tablets (Android and iOS)	Free in beta for Android; $9.99 for iOS	branchfire.com/ iannotate
Nitro Reader	PDF reader with collaboration, PDF creation, image and text extraction, form filling	Free	nitroreader.com
PDF Converter Free	PDF to PowerPoint converter from the Mac App Store	Free	wondershare.net
PDF Expert	**PDF tool to read, sign, annotate and organize PDFs on iOS devices**	**$9.99**	**readdle.com**
PDF Reader Pro	Mobile iOS app to create, annotate, scan and convert PDFs	$5.99	yuyao.com
PDF Toolkit +	**Mac app for splitting, merging, extracting pdf files**	**$1.99** $1.99	**In the App Store**

Security Check: PDF Conversion Sites

If you Google "convert PDF to Word online," you'll find a whole host of sites with names like, well, www.convertpdftoword.com (not a real site). I used to use these sites all the time, but I started getting uncomfortable about their ownership and the safety of my information. They're easy to use and ubiquitous; but if you find a site you want to use, I'd scan their privacy policy, make sure you know and trust the company, and watch what you upload.

Flowcharts and Diagramming Software

Apache OpenOffice Draw

Creately

draw.io

Gliffy

LibreOffice Draw

LucidChart

I think I can count on one hand the number of times I've needed a flowchart. My former publisher used to make them all the time; but it went out of business, so read anything you want to into that.

Even though I don't see a need for them in my business, they can be super handy for business organization charts, decision trees and floor plans. Microsoft Visio is a commercial product that many use; but I was surprised at the number of quality, free and bargain diagramming tools I discovered.

OpenOffice and LibreOffice business suites both include programs called **Draw,** which serve as flowchart and diagramming software. They're very similar in functionality, mainly because the two suites have the same roots. Another program, **draw.io,** lets you instantly start designing online without having to download anything.

Although it's handy to have a program to do your own diagrams, perhaps a more useful diagramming tool is one that lets you collaborate with others.

One of my readers' favorites is **Gliffy,** a web-based tool that makes it easy for you to create, share and collaborate with diagrams. **Creately** and **LucidChart** are similar, and they all have limited free plans that allow collaboration and sharing.

Flowcharts and Diagramming Software at a Glance

(recommended tools in **bold**)

Apache OpenOffice Draw	Downloadable diagramming software	Free	openoffice.org
Creately	Online diagram collaboration tool for flowcharts and wireframes	Free for limited diagrams (public only), or starting at $49/year for unlimited	creately.com
draw.io	**Free, instant online flowchart maker**	**Free**	**draw.io**
Gliffy	Online flowchart software with apps for Microsoft Office	Free for basic, or paid levels start at $5/month/user	gliffy.com
LibreOffice Draw	Downloadable diagramming software	Free	libreoffice.org
LucidChart	Online flowchart software with plug-ins and apps for many suites	Free version gives up to 60 elements, or starting at $3.33/ month for yearly subscription	lucidchart.com

Chapter 4

Website Tools

In this chapter:

Y ears ago when I was single, I was corresponding with a guy from an Internet dating site. Though we hadn't met, he decided I was worth pursing and declared me "the sexiest woman on the planet." I wrote a post about it (nerdy.bz/sexynerd) using that phrase as much as I could, pretending that Google would notice and validate me by ranking the post high in its search engine.

Boy was I shocked when it worked! For more than a year, I showed up on the first page of search results when you Googled "the sexiest woman on the planet" (with the quotation marks). For a while, I was No. 2, just after Scarlett Johansson; and even five years later, Google still has me listed on Page 3. Still sexy after all these years, I guess.

The point of this story is not to brag (although I want as many people in the world as possible to know that I'm still ranked as "the sexiest woman on the planet")—it's to talk about the importance of web analytics in keeping your website strong in the rankings and helpful for your visitors. On sites with very moderate traffic (like mine when I haven't posted a new free tool lately), it can be incredibly boring. But when I send out a newsletter or one of my tools goes viral for a few minutes on Twitter, I can discover cool things about the way people are using my site and perhaps insight into how I can make it more user-friendly.

Website Analytics

Chartbeat

ClickTale

Clicky

Google Analytics

Piwik

I will never claim to be an expert in web analytics, but I can say without hesitation that **Google Analytics** is one of the best tools in the universe to help you figure out what you need to know about your website. Use your Google account to generate code for each site; and within minutes, you'll be receiving more information about your site and visitors than you ever thought possible.

It's always adding new functionality; and each time I check my stats, I'm amazed even more by the new features. My favorite improvement is the capability to see visitors on your site in real time. You see them arrive, switch pages, click around, then take off. A little creepy, I know; but it's vital information to see how people use your site.

Here's a sample of what you'll see:

- ✔ How people find your site
- ✔ How often they visit
- ✔ Where they hang out
- ✔ How long they spend looking around
- ✔ How they navigate your site
- ✔ What page they are on when they exit
- ✔ Where your visitors come from

Another cool thing about Google Analytics these days is that many tools link into the statistics to give you even more information. For example, I can include Google Analytics links in my NerdWords newsletter through MailChimp (Page 144) to track clicks and activities generated from newsletter recipients.

And, of course, Google Analytics gives you the critical information you need to see how your site ranks with the keywords — thus I'm able to see that 880 people have visited my site in search of "the sexiest woman on the planet" since the post first appeared.

You can check your stats on the go with Google's free mobile app for Android; but if you're on an Apple product, you can find many third-party access apps. I could write a whole chapter on its statistics. In fact, a search on Amazon.com turned up almost 200 books that include info about Google Analytics, several of them dedicated to just that topic.

Chartbeat is an old favorite of mine because I first discovered Chartbeat when Ashton Kutcher and CNN were competing to be the first Twitter account with 1 million followers. Chartbeat showed the race live, and I was hooked with the magical changing numbers as real people clicked real buttons right before my eyes. **Clicky** and **ClickTale** give you fun graphics as well, and **Piwik** puts the statistics on your own computer with a downloadable program.

You can set up alerts so you get a text when a certain number of people visit your site at once, and the service sends you emails (or texts, your choice) when your site is down (which happens more than you know). The Chartbeat folks told me they chose the name because "Chartbeat is the heartbeat of your site, and we like charts!"

Website Analytics at a Glance
(recommended tools in **bold**)

Chartbeat	Real-time monitoring of all kinds of cool metrics	$9.95/month to monitor up to 1,000 active page views on up to 5 sites	chartbeat.com
ClickTale	Analytics tool with heatmaps and visitor activity recordings	Free for up to 400 visits a month then mystery pricing	clicktale.com
Clicky	Free basic analytics for up to 3,000 daily views	Basic free version, or starting at $9.99/month for lots of goodies	clicky.com
Google Analytics	**Best free website**	**Free**	**google.com/ analytics**
Piwik	Open-source, downloadable alternative to Google Analytics	Free	piwik.org

Blogs and Website Builders

Blogger

Checkthis

IM-Creator

SnapPages

Squarespace

Tumblr

Wix

WordPress

I'm not even going to pretend that I would consider any other blogging or website platform over **WordPress,** but I'd be selfish if I didn't at least mention some of the other great tools out there. These tools range from sites that are super easy drag-and-drop web builders to on-the-go blog and instant publishing tools that make it easy to collect and share content.

WordPress sites have come a long way. When the company opened its doors in 2003, it offered the earliest of blogs, simple sites that allowed you to write and share snippets of your life online. As blogging grew, so did the value of these types of sites; and search engines took notice. Before long, the dynamic nature of the content on a blog was attracting more search-engine attention than static websites. And when WordPress blogs became a part of regular sites, the sites (and companies behind them) benefited greatly.

Starting a WordPress blog or website is easy, for both personal and business use. For a free hosted site with a URL such as nerdybestfriend.wordpress.com, simply create an account and pick a name at WordPress.com. There, you can also purchase various upgrades, including a custom URL if you want your blog or site to live at nerdybestfriend.com. If you want total control—including a custom URL, a wide variety of plug-ins and the capability to sell your own advertising—you can download the free WordPress software from WordPress.org; but you must arrange and pay for hosting of the site.

The next step in building your site with WordPress is choosing a theme (Page 173), and here's where the magic begins. For less than $50, you can buy an easy-to-install framework for a full site, complete with the embedded blog for dynamic content, or not. You can further personalize your site with any of the thousands of plug-ins and widgets to do everything from embed video to automatically tweet your posts to Twitter to install a carousel-type photo gallery.

If you don't want to use WordPress, we're lucky these days to have myriad user-friendly website builders. You will frequently find an ad-supported free version, as well as pricing that starts at less than $10 a month and includes a free domain name and hosting. In addition, these types of services may also integrate robust site analytics plus an instant mobile version of your new site. Not a bad set of features for a do-it-yourself site!

I played around with four sites, and **IM-Creator** stood out to me as the one with the most interesting layouts and templates. And I like **Square-space** because it allows you to import other blogs so you don't lose your content. **SnapPages** is handy for its drag-and-drop functionality, and **Wix** is just plain easy.

And let's say you want to make an announcement but don't have time to contact your IT team or web guy to create another page on your website. **Checkthis** is perfect. It's a super-fast online poster creator that lets you create a one-page message. You can embed a poll or other tools, customize the look and have a cool, professional online presence up and running in minutes. The site has interactive features à la Facebook, allowing people to comment, share and adore your poster.

Blogger is another incredibly popular blogging platform; but I've always disliked it because it adds a link from your blog to the next Blogger site, and I was always afraid that the next one in line would be bad porn (as opposed to good porn?) or, heaven forbid, an anti-cupcake site.

When blogging and full-on websites just seem like too much work, you might try the instant gratification of a microblogging site. **Tumblr** in particular has become incredibly popular, although I've been hesitant to give it a try since I really don't need another site to have to update. Because of its popularity, you'll find that other platforms (such as "real" sites) can easily integrate Tumblr and other feeds into the pages so your updates appear anywhere you have a web presence.

Blog and Website Builders at a Glance (recommended tools in **bold**)

Blogger	Blog-building site	Free	blogger.com
Checkthis	**Online poster builder with interactive and social media elements**	**Free**	**checkthis.com**
IM-Creator	**Drag-and-drop website builder with cooler templates**	**Free with IM Creator branding, or starting at $7.95/month**	**imcreator.com**
SnapPages	**Drag-and-drop website builder**	**Free options abound; paid starts at $8/month**	**snappages.com**
Squarespace	Drag-and-drop website builder	Starts at $8/month	squarespace.com
Tumblr	Microblogging site	Free	tumblr.com
Wix	Drag-and-drop website builder with HTML5	Many templates and options for free; premium plans start at $50/year	wix.com
WordPress	**Best website and blog builder**	**Free blog at WordPress.com, or install WordPress software for total control**	**wordpress.com (free blog) wordpress.org (free software)**

Live Chat Website Add-Ons

BoldChat

LiveAgent Chat

Olark

OnlineChatCenters

Zopim

I am completely an UN-fan of websites with pop-ups, music, obnoxious auto-play videos and all those other annoyances. That being said, adding a live chat option to your website can provide your visitors with instant answers and your business with better relationships. **Zopim** is one of those little live chat boxes that sits on a website and gives you the chance to connect with your visitors as they browse your site. I installed it a couple of years ago with a WordPress plug-in, and I have to say I'm in love.

When I send out NerdWords on Friday, I make sure I'm around to be able to chat when people stop by. Frequently, I'll see the same folks stop by my site and say hello. It's like a virtual coffee shop with no coffee. Or cupcakes.

Zopim makes the chat easy because it integrates with my Google Chat service. I get a "clunk" sound when someone hits the site, and they see a message that I'm online. I prefer the passive presence, which means that I don't pop up and bother visitors when they arrive—they can talk to me if they want.

Most of the time, I use Zopim from my Gmail page. I have to set my status to "Available"; and I sometimes forget to change it back to "Invisible," which means I look like I'm online but away from the desk. If I really had my stuff together, I'd keep Zopim open on my phone through its apps, but I walk around staring at my phone enough without adding yet another task that keeps me nose down into my devices.

If I want more options, I can log in to the Zopim dashboard to see even more details. Zopim gives me a few details about the visitors, such as where they're from and what they're looking at; but other than that, I don't have any information unless they reach out to me. Then I set the service to require a first and last name so I don't have to write, "And to whom am I typing?"

If I am not around, I leave a friendly message in the chat box that encourages people to send a note. I probably get two-thirds of my weekly messages through that box.

Here's the most important thing I love about Zopim: It's 100 percent free for one user. It doesn't even put a note on the chat area that I'm using the free version. Having this feature makes me feel, I don't know, more official or something. It's a fancy addition that doesn't cost me anything but upgrades my profile and makes my website more useful to my visitors.

There are, of course, numerous Zopim competitors out there, many with free versions. But I love a company that starts with "Z"; and I've never had a lick of a problem with this service, so I'm a huge fan and a loyal customer. **BoldChat's** free version lets you have three concurrent conversations—up to 750 per month. You can have five at once on **Olark,** but only 20 per month. **OnlineChatCenters** matches Zopim's offer of unlimited chats for one operator, but its full version is much cheaper at $5/month. And if you're really into the whole interaction thing, **LiveAgent Chat** is a one-time price of $299 for a help desk/chat tool with integrated social media. Whichever one you go with, you're probably going to make better connections (and we hope more money) when you add this type of personal touch to your site.

Live Chat Providers at a Glance

(recommended tools in **bold**)

BoldChat	Live chat service for more than 1 site with 3 concurrent chats up to 750 per month	Free level, or advanced features starting at $99/year	boldchat.com
LiveAgent Chat	Multi-function help desk/ customer relationship tool with live chat	One-time payments start at $299 for live chat, online forum structure and social media help platforms	liveagentchat.com
Olark	Live chat service with up to 5 chat windows and 20 chats per month for free	Basic free version; other levels start at $17/month, or less for longer subscriptions	olark.com
OnlineChat Centers	Live chat service with 1 operator on 1 site with unlimited concurrent chats for free	Free for 1 operator and unlimited chats on 1 site; premium levels start at $5/month	onlinechatcenters.com
Zopim	**My favorite live chat service**	**Free for 1 operator and 1 concurrent chat; paid levels start about $14/month**	**zopim.com**

This book is interactive!
Scan with the Layar App for
updates, bonus material and more

More Website Tools

Down for Everyone or Just Me
UserTesting.com

These two tools don't really go together, but I find them handy and wanted to share.

One time I was showing my client his new site, and ARGHHH! It was down! We pasted his web address into **Downforeveryoneorjustme.com** and discovered that it was just a problem with my connection, not his site. We both breathed a sigh of relief.

Down for Everyone or Just Me? is a service of Site5 web hosting. When you find out if your site is down, Site5 flashes a message, "We guarantee our uptime! Switch to Site5 hosting!" Sometimes I'm tempted to take it up on the offer.

UserTesting.com is another helpful site when you're working on your web presence. For about $50, you can ask a complete stranger (someone who is not your mom) to walk through your site and give feedback. It's awesome to have a fresh set of eyes, especially if you've been staring at the site and tweaking it to death and can no longer be objective.

More Website Tools at a Glance

(recommended tools in **bold**)

Down for Everyone or Just Me	Site that checks to see if a site is done (or if it's just you)	Free	downforeveryoneorjustme.com
UserTesting.com	Testing and site walkthrough by real users	$49 for a video and report from a site reviewer	usertesting.com

Behind the Glasses:
Website Tools and Platforms

Here is a short list of the tools and services I use to keep my website running.

✔ Web hosting from Bluehost.com

✔ Premium WordPress templates from sites including WooThemes and Themeforest (Page 174)

✔ Integrated newsletter sign-ups with MailChimp (Page 144)

✔ Automations that publish all new posts to Facebook through IFTTT (Page 93)

✔ Live Chat software from Zopim (Page 50)

✔ On-demand technical help from a WordPress expert on Fiverr (Page 247)

Chapter 5

Task and Project Management

Applications, software and systems that help you keep track of what you have to do both alone and with groups. Boy howdy, but that's a crowded, crowded, crowded field. I looked at some of the top lists to try to share the most-revered programs; and even if a group had narrowed the list to five or 10, I found 50+ more programs in the comments below the post. So, although I'm going to attempt to write about the top task and project management tools here, keep in mind that you may not find your favorite among them. And also note that although I talk about the features that differentiate them, they add features faster than I can type; and new "best ever!" task management apps pop up every week, more often than the latest celebrity diet book.

Task Management

Choosing a task management system is a personal thing. It's kind of like what some doctors say when recommending a diet—the perfect diet is the one that works for you. People choose their favorites based on any number of factors, such as:

- ✔ "I put all my stuff into this app when it first came out, and it'll take too long to switch."
- ✔ "I need one that integrates with Dropbox and Evernote."
- ✔ "I like the location-based apps that ding me at the grocery store to remind me to pick up milk."
- ✔ "I have to have something that works on Android, iOS, Mac, PC and Linux!"

As you search for the perfect system for you, peruse this list of features and options:

- ✔ **System complexity**

   Some to-do lists are just that—lists. You write something down and check it off, like **Google Tasks,** or create simple lists on a blank page, like **WorkFlowy.** These are great for people like me who just want to make sure we don't forget anything but don't want to spend a lot of time messing around with organization. Other systems are much more complex. They let you tag and categorize tasks or let you assign priorities, such as the much-loved **Wunderlist.**

✔ **Philosophy**

Many of the task systems rely on an underlying school of thought for time management. In 2002, a successful business-man named David Allen published *Getting Things Done* and changed the lives of millions of people. He developed a concrete system of prioritizing tasks and setting goals with straightfor-ward rules and organized folders. If you're a *GTD* fan, many systems can be configured to follow his philosophy, such as **Things.** If you adore your FranklinCovey day planner and organization system, you have **Opus Domini** apps and soft-ware. And you can choose the downloadable **PomodoroApp** based on the Pomodoro Technique developed by Francesco Cirillo. When you're choosing your own task list manager, you may want to try out the different techniques to see what works best for your life.

✔ **Collaboration**

Some systems are made for your eyes only, while others special-ize in helping teams track projects and tasks (see project man-agement systems, Page 61). As you do your research, check to make sure that the task-sharing tools you need are included in the level you want to pay for because sometimes the teamwork options are only available in paid versions.

✔ **Accessibility**

Many of these systems have apps and programs for both the yin and the yang. You'll find systems that let you control your lists from any possible device, as well as downloadable programs that only work on your PC or Mac. You should also consider how you want to add and delete tasks to your lists. Some let you tweet them in, call them in, email them in and use dictation, or use shortcuts in messaging to categorize on the fly, such as **Producteev.**

✔ **GPS functionality**

Do you need a reminder to pick up the milk when you're driving by the store? You can find systems such as **Toodledo** that poke you with a text or other reminder based on your location, kind of like a helpful backseat driver.

✔ **Integrations and add-ons**

If you love Evernote (Page 104) or have files in Dropbox (Page 8), you'll find that many systems talk to your other applications to make sure you have all you need to stay organized, like the way **Any.DO** connects with Gmail to let you turn any email into a task.

✔ **Appearance and interface**

The **Clear** apps for iOS and Macs are absolutely gorgeous, a gradient rainbow of color with each task on a line of its own. **Remember The Milk** has been around since 2004 and has a dozen ways to sort, organize, view and configure the way you see your tasks. When you seek out the perfect system, you'll find a tremendous variety of looks and interfaces that give you options for colors, backgrounds and interaction gestures.

Task Management Tools at a Glance

Because these tools and apps tend to add features and change pricing structure more often than Lindsay Lohan goes to court, I'm going to simply list some of the top tools in this category instead of creating the regular chart.

Any.Do	any.do
Clear	**realmacsoftware.com/clear**
Google Tasks	mail.google.com/Tasks
Memo to Me	memotome.com
Opus Domini	piso13.com
PomodoroApp	pomodoroapp.com
Producteev	producteev.com
Remember The Milk	rememberthemilk.com
TaskLabels	tasklabels.com
Things	culturedcode.com/things
Toodledo	toodledo.com
WorkFlowy	worklowy.com
Wunderlist	**wunderlist.com**

NerdHerd Favorite: TaskLabels

Holly C. uses **TaskLabels** on her iPad and PC to "arrange my tasks under different categories and easily see what needs to be done each day."

Behind the Glasses:
The Way I Get Things Done

I'm ashamed to admit that my task management system has always been a pen and a pad—a steno pad, to be precise. I put the date in the top right corner (spelled out, of course) and fill both columns of the page with a numbered list with bullets as the second-level tasks. Unlike most diets I've tried, the system works for me; and no matter how many times I signed up for the next great to-do list software, I reverted to the pad.

But in 2013, my assistant, Rachel, and I needed a better way to keep track of tasks for upcoming speaking engagements. So I downloaded pretty much every tool in this chapter to see what would work best for us. **Astrid** seemed like the winner. I could assign tasks to Rachel right from Gmail, and it automatically included the first few lines of the email with the task. We could leave each other notes on tasks. Astrid worked everywhere on every device. And it was free.

Whoopee! A task system that worked! We were happily tasking each other back and forth for about a month until my Whoopee! turned into a Yahoo!—as in Yahoo! the company, which bought Astrid and shut it down. It took a few weeks to find a new system, but Teambox (Page 67) is a clear winner.

NerdHerd Favorite: Memo to Me

Eva Lang remembers important events with a simple reminder service called **Memo to Me**, which lets you set multiple reminders for a week event. "For a birthday, you could have a reminder a week in advance so you can send the card, and then another reminder on the day itself."

Project Management

Not so very long ago, project management was a very complicated thing. Companies would hire project managers, frequently people with advanced degrees who were trained to coordinate with all the doers and approvers and money-spenders on a project to get work completed on time and on budget. The projects they talked about were BIG ones: building a rocket, buying a company, rolling out a new product. The project manager would use specialized software (such as Microsoft Project) to identify resources, tasks and timetables; and then the project manager would take care of assigning the jobs and checking up on people. There were these mysterious graphics called Gantt charts that were supposed to show the progress of the project, but really only the project manager knew how to create and read them.

But more and more smaller organizations just needed to figure out how to coordinate projects that didn't involve rocket scientists. They needed to bring together designers, committee members and department heads to revamp websites. They needed to organize conferences or collaborate on end-of-the-year reports for the boards.

Thus began an era of what I like to call "Project Management for the Rest of Us." Software companies used the web as a gathering place for to-do lists, action items, resource libraries and communication. Setting up the project was easy to do for the average computer user, and groups could break down the projects into their components to make sure everyone did his part.

These days, dozens of companies now offer fairly low-cost ways for groups to work together remotely and in the office to get things done. This section covers a variety of vendors, from the pioneers in this space to the startups.

Simple Project Management Tools

Basecamp

Smartsheet

Tom's Planner

Trello

Although these basic project management tools are adding more and more functionality, they're more straightforward than the tools in the business workflow section (Page 63). We must start with the project management system that really kicked off the do-it-yourself project management trend. In 2004, a company called 37signals started creating online project management systems, primarily for the web design industry. **Basecamp** has evolved to be one of the most popular web-based project collaboration tools to share files, meet deadlines, assign tasks, centralize feedback and finish what you start.

Basecamp is now integrated with a whole host of other systems, including time tracking software, social networks, mobile phones and invoicing software. All the systems update each other and keep everyone on track. Basecamp has toyed off and on with a free level; but as of early June 2013, its smallest plan gives you 15 projects for $1/day.

A fellow nerd who attended one of my sessions swears by **Smartsheet,** a simple project management tool for people who love spreadsheets. It's easy to use and understand, and it works in a linear fashion that makes sense. If you are one of the rare people who can figure out Gantt charts, you might try **Tom's Planner,** which starts at $9/month for 20 "project schedules."

Trello offers an interesting take on project management by organizing your projects into "cards" that lay out like a deck across your screen. You can click on any card to flip it over and see the details, including tasks, collaborators and due dates. And another cool Trello characteristic? It's 100 percent free.

NerdHerd Thumbs Up: Smartsheet

Chris Champion from the Institute of Public Works Engineering Australia says Smartsheet is a great collaboration tool that can also manage file attachments and discussion notes.

Business Workflow Tools

Asana

Do

Podio

Hands down, this has been the toughest segment to write in this entire book. The problem is that these tools, properly and fully utilized, could truly revolutionize my business—and yours as well, especially if you work with a small team and are responsible for getting things done. The dangerous phrase above is "properly and fully utilized" because getting the most out of these tools is going to take some serious work.

At their core, they are project management tools for groups. Like the more straightforward tools in this chapter, they allow you to set up projects, create and assign tasks, set milestones, adhere to deadlines, and take a project to its completion.

But all of these tools go much further than that. The tool that looks the most interesting, at least for my needs, is **Podio,** which combines the project management systems with integrated modules (it calls them "apps") that extend the functionality to cover almost everything you could possibly do in a business.

On the simple side, you can track time and keep schedules, just like you can with many of the simple tools. But from there, the possibilities look truly infinite. Here are a few of the things you can do with Podio:

✔ Create a customer relationship management (CRM) system (see Page 140) to help you and your colleagues track leads and conversations

✔ Integrate your products and sales into your projects

✔ Institute an employee reward and "attaboy" program that gives them kudos for achievements

✔ Establish a living library of shared documents

✔ Keep up with the activities of your business through a social media-type update page

✔ Customize workflows and activity lists to fit your business model

✔ Capture institutional knowledge in shared wikis

Podio is priced very reasonably, especially for small teams. Five or fewer active team members are free, and then you'll pay $9/user per month. The problem with the system is not the price—it's the time it'll take you to personalize Podio to make it do everything you want it to. Podio lists several partner companies that will customize the system for you, but a quick call to one partner revealed a price range of $1,000 to $30,000 for the service. That probably translates into 10 to 50 hours minimum on your end if you want to do it yourself. Setting up Podio for basic services takes as little time as an hour; but to maximize the functionality, I think you'll need a Christmas break with no email, lots of cupcakes and the time to really think things through.

Asana and **Do** are somewhat similarly equipped to streamline your business processes. Do is a Salesforce product (Page 140), which means it integrates directly into that CRM. It can also act as a business deal tracker, a template repository and a contact manager for groups. Do's free version limits you to 10 deals and 1,000 contacts, but its full version is more price-friendly than Podio at about $5/user per month.

Asana is actually more popular than Podio, drawing accolades from big-name bloggers and other important reviewers. You can use Asana for project management, CRM, bug tracking and applicant tracking. I like that it has a video library with tutorials on different uses. It has a free plan for groups of less than 30, then pricing starts at $100/month.

NerdHerd Thumbs Up: Podio

Lissa W. Clayborn from the Computer Science Teachers Association thinks Podio is great for collaboration, storage, meeting planning and project management.

Project Management Tools at a Glance (recommended tools in **bold**)

Asana	Free project and team management system for up to 30 collaborators	Free for up to 30 members, or starting at $100/month	asana.com
Basecamp	**The pioneer in online project management**	**Starter plan gives you 15 projects for $1/day**	**basecamp.com**
Do	Salesforce's project management and business workflow tool	Free level for unlimited projects and tasks with 1,000 contacts and 10 deals, or paid plans start at $15/month for 3 group members and unlimited deals and contacts	do.com
Podio	**Work management system with project management, CRM functionality, meeting features and real-time collaboration**	**Free for up to 5 team members, then $9/month/user**	**podio.com**
Smartsheet	Project management tool for spreadsheet fans	Starts at $9.95/month	smartsheet.com
Teambox	**Online project management and collaboration tool with Google and Dropbox integration**	**Free for 5 projects, or paid plans start at $25/month**	**teambox.com**
Tom's Planner	Online Gantt chart software that allows anyone to create, collaborate and share Gantt charts	Free for 1 project, or paid plans start at $9/month	tomsplanner.com
Trello	Project management and collaboration tool with cool card interface	Free	trello.com

NerdHerd Favorite: Teambox

Amy Williams from Association Headquarters, Inc., loves **Teambox**, an online project management and collaboration tool. "Teambox has so many great features beyond collaborative project management, such as file sharing, whiteboards, Google and Dropbox integration and video conferencing, to name a few!"

Nerdy Tip: Top Trends in Task Management Systems

In the time it takes to read this chapter, the task and project management apps in this book will have added five new features. Zoom! There's another one! The apps that compete with each other work very hard to outdo—and copy—each other, so they are all engaged in raising the bar higher and higher.

Here are some trends you'll see as you peruse these tools:

✔ **Integrations, integrations, integrations**

Rather than making you upload files into a system, many of these tools are integrating with other services, such as Dropbox, Evernote and Gmail. This lets you share data and other items without having to duplicate the work.

✔ **On-the-go everything**

These apps aren't shy about building more apps. You should be able to find mobile access from any number of smart devices, no matter what platform you have.

✔ **Awesomeness you'll have to pay for**

If you're going to really make use of the full value of these robust tools, be prepared to pay for it. If you're a light user, you might be able to get by on the free versions. But these guys are counting on you becoming dependent on the advanced features that require a monthly fee.

✔ **Social media lookalikes**

We've become very used to the idea of social feeds because of Facebook and Twitter. Many of these tools will include dashboards with activity feeds to let you see recent happenings at a glance. In addition, we'll be seeing more of our social media activities pulled into our project management home pages to track what's happening in our social media outside world.

✔ **Tools that bring tools together**

The section on automation (Page 93) talks about many of the tools that help link your task managers with the tools you need to complete your tasks. Look for more of these cloud bridge tools to help you pull together your critical work areas.

Chapter 6

Efficiency Tools

Wouldn't it be easier if things were, well, easier? If you didn't have to jump through hoops to get your files, or type everything out, or explain what's on your screen?

These tools are the save-your-hide resources that eliminate roadblocks and make your workday go more smoothly.

Remote Access Tools

Chrome Remote Desktop
GoToMyPC
LogMeIn
Splashtop

Before I moved all my files to the cloud with Dropbox, I used to depend on **LogMeIn** to keep me connected to my main computer when I was on the road. This allowed me to access Microsoft Outlook (until I moved to Gmail, Page 103), keep track of my time with WorkTime (Page 91) and, in general, keep myself grounded.

LogMeIn is similar to the very popular GoToMyPC; but LogMeIn Free is, well, free. The tools allow you to use another computer to access your main machine, letting you control the device just like you were sitting in front of it with minimal lag time as long as you have a pretty robust Internet connection on both sides. The tools also let you access files, give control to someone else (like the teenage nephew who can fix your computer), and even play multimedia files remotely.

You'll find other tools in this category; and many of them also include mobile access tools, letting you control your computer from your smartphone to find a file for your assistant while you're standing in line to board a plane. **GoToMyPC** is about $10/month; and the pro version of LogMeIn, which is helpful if you need the service frequently, is $70/year.

That's not very much for such a convenient capability, right? Well, what if it were completely free? **Google's Chrome Remote Desktop** tool lives in the Chrome browser (or on Chrome PCs) and offers pretty much the same capability for free, including the capability to cut and paste info from your remote computer to the one you're using to access it. On Windows machines, you can also listen to audio files in real time.

But the biggest breakthrough tool may be **Splashtop,** a remote-access tool with a lot of splashy coolness. The free version gives you the capability to remote into your computers from any device on the same Wi-Fi network. For just $10/year, you can remote in from devices not connected to the same network.

Security Alert: Remote Access Concerns

Stop! Download not until you read further!

Before you get all excited about being able to access your desktop computer from anywhere, let's talk security. The Verizon 2012 Data Breach Investigations Report revealed that 88 percent of security breaches came from a weak password protocol coupled with installed remote access tools.

What does that mean? It means if you're using wimpy passwords and lazy security habits, plus you have some of these cool remote-access tools, you may be an open book for hackers. So before you start playing around with these tools, head over to the chapter on Computer Tools and Utilities (Page 15) and take steps to lock down your computer security.

Remote-Access Tools at a Glance (recommended tools in **bold**)

Chrome Remote Desktop	Remote-access tool for Chrome browser and PCs	Free	Available in the Chrome Web Store
GoToMyPC	Remote-access tool	Starts at $9.95/month	gotomypc.com
LogMeIn	Remote-access tool with robust free version	Free for basic, or Pro for $69.95/year for 1 computer	logmein.com
Splashtop	**Remote-access tool designed for mobile devices**	**Free for personal or $100/user/year for business**	**splashtop.com**

Voice Recognition Systems

Way back in the early days of voice recognition, here's what a dictation session sounded like with my 1997 version of **Dragon NaturallySpeaking.**

> I say: "I want a cupcake."
>
> Dragon writes: "The man picked up the rake."
>
> I say: "Delete that."
>
> Dragon writes: "Deplete cats."
>
> I say: "CHANGE THAT!"
>
> Dragon writes: "Change bats."
>
> I scream: "STOP IT!"
>
> Dragon writes: "You started it."

Lordy but I hated that blankety-blank program.

To train the system to recognize your voice, you had to read multiple passages during setup, then you had to keep training as you tried to work. I say "tried" because most of my time was spent starting with half a sentence, seeing Dragon make an error, then repeating, "DELETE THAT; CHANGE THAT; DELETE THAT" until the program got it right. I gave up on Dragon within a month after I spent an entire Saturday morning determined to make it work and ended up hoarse, angry and fed up.

Flash forward more than 15 years; and speech recognition is almost effortless, on both your computers and your mobile devices.

Speech Recognition Technology

Built-in Mac and Windows Speech Recognition

Dragon Products

Google Search

I'm comfortable saying that Nuance's **Dragon** software programs are the tip top of any list of speech recognition technology. Dragon products really type what you say—without hours of training or cursing. Nuance has been around the longest, it's gobbled up lots of competitors, and it has the widest variety of tools in this area. Dragon computer software is not free; but if you're in need of a tool that will type as you text, it's worth the investment (starting at $100).

If you want to go the free route, both Mac and Windows include free speech recognition systems in their operating systems. They're good for quick dictations and perhaps navigating through programs, but neither is a heavy-duty tool for extensive dictation. **Google search** in the Chrome browser includes a handy speech recognition tool that allows you to speak your search to find instant results.

Mobile Speech Recognition Tools

Dragon Apps

EVA and EVAN

Google Now

Maluuba

Siri

Skyvi

For voice recognition on the go, we have **Siri,** a pleasantly perky voice recognition system built into the iPhone. You can speak to **Siri** as if she were a personal assistant or even a friend, and she translates commands and questions into actions easily and with amazing accuracy.

Siri has a number of competitors for many mobile platforms, all with their own specialties and weaknesses. On Android devices, the top personal assistant tools are **Maluuba, Skyvi** and the **EVA and EVAN** "twin" apps so you can choose a male or female personality.

Dragon is also a big player in this area, with apps that do a variety of specialized tasks for iOS, Android and even BlackBerry devices. Unlike the desktop software, the **Dragon** apps are free.

Google Now has a huge advantage over, well, everything in the Android market. In addition to being a serious Siri-competitor, perhaps a victor, Google Now integrates your personal search history into "cards" of information, which are displayed at your command, when and where you need them.

For example, on your morning commute, a card might show your commute time and an alternate route to avoid traffic. You can get a report of how many miles you drove or walked/ran each month. If you're a sports fan, Google Now might feed up cards with up-to-date scores and news. And if you're headed to the airport, Google Now may help you pull up your boarding pass and show you the weather at your destination. And if you've been searching the web for Kim Kardashian news, you may get an automatic update if she announces a pregnancy, divorce or prison sentence.

Security Alert: Google and Privacy

My thoughts on Google Now: Are we ready to have a machine (and the company behind that machine) know that much about us? I suppose I'm naive to think that it doesn't already know that stuff, but perhaps I would rather remain a little in the dark about the information I'm providing.

I say that, but even without Google Now, Google knows and tracks an awful lot about me. In 2009, Google CEO Eric Schmidt said, "If you have something that you don't want anyone to know, maybe you shouldn't be doing it in the first place." And if you are doing it, you can bet that someone at Google probably knows about it. Google consistently commands about 67 percent of the search engine space, with the second place competitor, China-based Baidu, grabbing less than 9 percent. Most of the information Google (and other search engines) collects helps it target you with ads. (You wouldn't believe how many bakery shop offers show up on my pages.) But you can fly a little lower under the radar by taking a few privacy steps.

1. Log in to your Google account at google.com/history to see all your Google history. You can select items to be removed from your online life, but it'll still keep the info on file somewhere for several months.

2. Use a variety of search engines instead of just one so your whole online discovery is not visible on one page.

3. Use a browser's incognito mode to search, well, incognito.

Speech Recognition Tools at a Glance (recommended tools in **bold**)

Dragon Apps	Multiple apps for iOS, Android and BlackBerry for dictation and mobile assistant functionality	Free	nuancemobilelife.com/apps
Dragon Software	**Multiple software programs for Mac and PC for dictation and voice control**	**Starting at $100**	**nuance.com/dragon**
EVA and EVAN	Male and female personal mobile assistants for Android with special Car Mode for driving	Free "intern" versions available, or $19.99 for full	bulletproof.com
Google Now	Android-based personal assistant with significant data connections	Free	google.com/landing/now
Google Voice search	**Voice recognition feature for searching Google with Google Chrome browser**	**Free (only in Chrome browser)**	**google.com**
Maluuba	Mobile personal assistant for Windows and Android devices	Free	maluuba.com
Siri	**Personal assistant feature built in to iOS devices**	**Free**	**apple.com/ios/siri**
Skyvi	Android-based personal assistant with a sense of humor	Free	skyviapp.com

Behind the Glasses:
Five Ways I Use Siri

1. **Magnificent multitasking**

   While I'm setting up a room before a presentation, I can plow through a few emails by dictating as I walk around.

2. **Safe texting**

   When I'm driving, I can send a quick text message using hands-free technology and Siri.

3. **Husband pleasing**

   When my poor husband has to leave a New England Patriots game to pick me up at the airport, I ask Siri to keep us updated on the score as we drive home, and D.J. is happy(ish).

4. **Quick calculating**

   Siri often serves as my calculator when it's too much of a pain to open the calculator app, or, heaven forbid, I try to do the math myself.

5. **Weather reporting**

   When I'm packing my bags for a speaking engagement, I'll ask Siri for the weather report for the next city.

Tips to Get the Most out of Voice Recognition

✔ **Garbage input = garbled output**
The most important factor in successful use of voice recognition tools is sound quality. If you're using Dragon software on your computer, invest in a quality headset instead of relying on the internal microphone. On the go with your mobile device, you should find a quiet place to speak into the microphone, and make sure you have a good signal.

✔ **Practice, practice, practice**
If you're dictating more than a sentence or two, you may find yourself hesitating and mixing up your sentences. The more time you spend practicing, the better you will be at getting your thoughts out without sending the software off in the wrong direction.

✔ **Recognize your composition style**
I would love to be able to dictate my blog posts, books and other writing; but it turns out that my more creative side flows better through my fingers than through my lips. Thus, I use speech-to-text software to create lists, write short emails, jot down notes and create other short pieces—not for longer writing projects that require a different type of mental organization.

Screencapture Tools

If I made a chart of the time I've saved from each category of tech tool, tools for screencapture—including video screencapture, called screencasting—would top the list. Here are a few of the ways they have truly revolutionized the way I work.

Steps to tell my web guy about a typo on my website:

Before Screencasting	After Screencasting
1. Press the Print Screen button on my keyboard.	1. Use a tool to capture the portion of the screen with the typo.
2. Create a new document in Microsoft Word.	2. Draw arrows to typo and add notes.
3. Paste screen.	3. Push button to send capture to Screencast.com. Online link is automatically generated and ready to paste.
4. Open picture editing tools to crop screen.	
5. Add notes.	
6. Save the document.	4. Open an email.
7. Open an email.	5. Write note, paste link and send.
8. Attach the document.	
9. Write a note and send.	

And wait, there's more! I also use these tools to:

- ✔ Grab graphics from the web

- ✔ Create computer process training videos, talking through a process while the computer captures every click of my mouse and keyboard

- ✔ Give feedback on documents without typing out all the comments

- ✔ Add notes and arrows to maps to make directions better

- ✔ Demo tech tools for my followers on YouTube

- ✔ Show people at help desks what happens when things go wrong with my computer

Video Screencaptures

FastStone

Jing

QuickTime

Screencast-O-Matic

Screencast.com

Screenium

Snagit

One of my favorite free tools of all time is **Jing,** a little application from Tech-Smith, which makes the screencapture process insanely easy. Jing sits on your screen at all times in the form of a little yellow sun. You can click on the capture button to bring up crosshairs that allow you to capture the part of the screen you want. Then you can either create an image that you can add notes to, or a movie up to five minutes long! It rocks.

Another cool thing? Once you have the capture you want, you can save it to your computer or toss it up to your own private account at **Screencast.com.** You can also upload it to Facebook or Twitter or simply copy and paste it into a document.

Snagit is Jing's big brother; and for the $50 price tag, you get extra features such as borders, stamps and the capability to capture scrolling screens. I upgraded to get one of my favorite features, a one-button upload to YouTube for video captures.

Another download, **FastStone Capture,** is made just for Windows. You can capture windows, the full screen, a scrolling screen and a video with audio. In addition, when you capture something, you get a whole host of editing options to add a little more flair and details.

FastStone has a couple of extra handy tools such as a screen magnifier plus a color picker (like Pixie, Page 190). FastStone has a number of ways to export your capture, but I still prefer Jing's integration with Screencast.com. But the new FastStone touchscreen functionality for Windows 8 seems pretty darn cool.

For Macs, there's also **Screenium,** which will capture your smiling face on webcam while you talk through your presentation. Because I frequently work from home, I turn off this feature—no one wants to see me in PJs. I also like that it will highlight your mouse as you move it. You can also set it to move the capture window with your mouse movements, so the screen zooms to whatever part of the screen you're working on. Plus, you can edit video in the software without having to export to another video editor.

And believe it or not, the free version of **QuickTime** on Macs includes screen recording. Sorry, PC folks—it's not available for Windows.

Screencast-O-Matic is super handy, but I shudder each time a program tries to run on Java these days. If you have Java enabled in your browser (which I don't), you simply go to the main page and click a button to instantly record what is on your screen—no downloads! The free version gives you all kinds of extras, such as including your webcam in the broadcast and animated mouse clicks. But if you don't pay the $15/year (which includes even more extras), you have to live with the company's watermark.

NerdHerd Thumbs Up: Jing

I'm not the only one who loves Jing. Cheryl Paglia from Textile Care Allied Trades Association says, "I love this thing. I can go to our members' websites and Jing their logo to use in our newsletter or on our website! I don't have to ask folks to send me pictures. If they have it on their website, I can get it!" And Leigh Ann Senoussi adds, "I use Jing almost every day!"

Screenshots

Awesome Screenshot

Skitch

Webpage Screenshot

Windows Snipping Tool

Skitch, a freebie from Evernote (Page 104), is my favorite app for on-the-go screenshots and annotations on my iPad. You can annotate a picture from your album, upload a PDF, annotate a screen snap of anything on your device, or capture a shot from the web. Then it's easy to add notes and share or save. I appreciate the pixelate feature that lets you blur out personal information — or an ex-boyfriend's face.

The Chrome Store has thousands of extensions you can add to your browser to make your life easier, including screenshot tools. After you install them, you can click the button from any webpage to grab a full screen or just a portion—even capture the whole webpage without scrolling.

My favorite is **Webpage Screenshot.** It's free, of course (always something that makes me love a tool more); and besides having all the standard screenshot features I look for, it also lets you edit a webpage before you capture it, meaning you can actually change the text on a published page. It made me a little uneasy to do it to my own site because I feared I was messing up the original page, but it's actually only a copy.

Another cool tool is called **Awesome Screenshot,** which has the same types of features plus the capability to create a temporary link so your share doesn't stay online forever. Awesome Screenshot is available on several browsers and comes from Diigo, a deluxe bookmarking tool.

NerdHerd Favorite: Windows Snipping Tool

The **Windows Snipping Tool** is a free utility included on Windows operating systems. According to Steven R. Jones from the Association of Cable Communicators, "This is a super easy-to-use tool that allows items to be saved in JPEG, PNG, GIF and HTML formats."

Screencapture Tools at a Glance   (recommended tools in **bold**)

Awesome Screenshot	Browser extension from Diigo for screenshots with temporary sharing capabilities	Free	awesomescreenshot.com
FastStone	Windows-based screencapture tool with support for touchscreens	$19.95	faststone.org
Jing	**My favorite screencapture tool ever!**	**Free**	**techsmith.com/jing**
QuickTime (Mac only)	Free screencapture tool hidden in the free version of QuickTime for Mac	Free	apple.com/quicktime
Reflector	**Download that mirrors your iPhone or iPad on your Mac or PC**	**$12.99**	**reflectorapp.com**
Screencast-O-Matic	Online screencast tool (runs with Java)	Free with watermark, or Pro version and more features for $15/year	screencastomatic.com
Screencast.com	Online storage for Jing and Snagit captures or anything else	Free for 2GB storage and 2GB bandwidth, or $9.95/month for more	screencast.com
Screenium	**Mac-based screencapture tool with webcam integration**	**$39.99**	**syniumsoftware.com/screenium**
Skitch	**Android and iOS app and desktop download from Evernote for annotated screenshots**	**Free**	**evernote.com/skitch**

Screencapture Tools at a Glance (continued)

Snagit	**Screencapture software from the makers of Jing**	**$49.95**	**techsmith.com/snagit**
Webpage Screenshot	Chrome extension for screenshots with web content editing and easy sharing	Free	webpagescreenshot.info
Windows Snipping Tool	Windows utility for screenshots	Free	Included in Windows software

Behind the Glasses:
Recording Mobile Device Screens

I feel like I use a secret app that should amaze people; but since no one has asked about it, the awesomeness of it must all in my head. But I still think it's pretty darn cool.

The secret app is **Reflector**, and it's a download for your desktop that wirelessly mirrors your iPhone or iPad on the screen. I use Reflector all the time to record screencasts of walkthroughs of the apps I use on my devices. Since there just aren't any quality apps that let you record your mobile device movements, connecting to my laptop through Reflector is the best option so far.

Of course, I could jailbreak my iPhone and use other tools like Reflector. Apple is very strict about its operating system and app library, and that makes some of my fellow nerds mad. So they developed a way to break down the security and permission walls in a device, a process they call "jailbreaking." Android devices are not as strict, but users routinely give themselves more permissions to customize their phones through a process called "rooting." In the United States at least, jailbreaking a device is not illegal, but providers threaten that doing so can be a violation of the warranty.

I just can't bring myself to jailbreak my iPhone because

1. I don't think most of my readers would jailbreak, and I try to mimic how you live, and

2. I'm pretty sure my mother would find out and ground me.

That being said, I know that there are a whole wealth of cool apps out there in jailbreak land that would greatly expand my collection, including tools that allow people to record the movements directly from their phones. But I'm fine with playing by the rules and buying my little workaround products like Reflector. It's what my mother would want.

This book is interactive!
Scan with the Layar App for updates, bonus material and more

Chapter 7

Time
Management Tools

In this chapter:

If technology itself were the key to productivity, we would all have our ducks in a row. I don't know about you; but some days, despite having thousands of apps and programs at my disposal, I'm still running around like a chicken, unorganized, distracted, unfocused and befuddled.

The key to managing your time is not necessarily to find a tool—it's to create or adopt a system then find the technology and other resources you need to support your system.

In this chapter, you'll find tools to manage task lists, schedules and time-sucking distractions, as well as a small section on what I use to keep my business running. If I come up with the perfect formula that will work for everyone, I'll let you know.

Calendars

Cozi Family Organizer

Fantastical

Google Calendar

Outlook.com Calendar

Rainlendar

Sunrise

Even though I go old school with my task lists (see Behind the Glasses, Page 60), I couldn't live without my synchronized calendars that track but hide personal appointments as well as share public events such as speaking engagements.

If you're implementing a full time-management system with task management and all the bells and whistles, you might want to use its internal calendar. Or you can use one of these to access and manage your private and public events. You may also use the calendar that comes with Microsoft Outlook or **Outlook.com.** Both versions let you import and export feeds to bring the appointments with you no matter where you are.

If you have a life outside the office, you may need **Cozi.** Cozi is a family-friendly calendaring tool that allows each member of a family (or office) to share schedules, synchronize lists and keep track of everything that needs keeping track of. In every presentation I give, someone starts smiling and shares how Cozi saved her family's sanity.

It also offers a number of other apps made for families, including the Family Locater, Sitter Manager, Password Vault and even a coloring book.

My main calendar of choice is **Google Calendar.** I access the calendar on my iOS devices with the attractive **Sunrise** app, which also pulls in my Facebook and LinkedIn events. Google Calendar serves as both my home base for appointments and the feed to schedules I need to track in other applications. It's one of those services I don't think I could live without.

With Google Calendar, you can create multiple calendars on the same system, so your personal events are marked in orange and work stuff turns up red. Any one of these calendars can be shared with the public as well as individuals, giving permission to view, edit or change as you desire. This allows me to share my work calendar with my assistant, who can add appointments, and my personal calendar with my husband, who can then figure out when I've signed up to run another half marathon.

What's more, you can import other RSS feeds as needed into the calendar, which makes it easy for me to track my presentations for different groups in a special application for speakers.

People love **Rainlendar** for desktop-based, nonsyncing schedules. I'm jealous of (and mystified by) these guys who feel secure enough to leave their work at work without constantly checking schedules via devices. Another downloadable favorite is **Fantastical** (for Apple products).

NerdHerd Favorite: Pocket Informant

Super Nerd Linda Chreno is always contributing awesome tools. She likes **Pocket Informant** to manage her calendars, tasks, notes and contacts on her desktop and on the go.

Calendars at a Glance

(recommended tools in **bold**)

Cozi Family Organizer	**Family-friendly calendar and task manager**	**Free for basic, or Cozi Gold for $29/year**	**cozi.com**
Fantastical	Mac-based calendar with iOS apps	$19.99	flexibits.com/ fantastical
Google Calendar	**Web-based calendar with import and export capabilities**	**Free**	**google.com/ calendar**
Outlook.com Calendar	Web-based Microsoft Outlook calendar	Free	outlook.com
Pocket Informant	Calendar and task tool for iOS and Android	$14.99	pocketinformant.com
Rainlendar	Downloadable desktop calendar for Windows and Mac	Free for Lite version, or 9.95 EUR for Pro	rainlendar.net
Sunrise	**iOS app that combines Facebook, LinkedIn and Google Calendar**	**Free**	**sunrise.im**

Time Management

KeepMeOut
LeechBlock
RescueTime
WorkTime

Do you ever look at the clock and say, "What the heck have I done for the past two hours?" Facebook, breaking news online, cupcakes in the break room—any number of distractions can keep you from being productive. In today's world, we have way too many tantalizing distractions that can pull us away from the things we have to do.

To keep a handle on these addictive habits, you can make use of several free tools that will put you back on track. You can find many tools that track time for you when you push a button; but if I'm too busy to think straight and rushing through my tasks, I certainly can't remember to turn a timer on and off for each project.

My sentimental time-tracking favorite happens to be the ugliest tech tool in this book; but, my friends, it just works. **WorkTime** by Nestersoft (for Windows only) tracks every single activity on your computer in six-second increments. It shows you how long you surf the web, work on a document, spend writing emails.

Like I said, it's not pretty, but it works. When I had a PC, I used it for years to track projects, identify distractions, evaluate workloads and, in general, get my stuff together.

In 2012, a blogger who uses another time-tracking tool, **RescueTime,** ran a report that showed him that he was wasting more than 60 percent of his time on Facebook and Reddit. So he hired a stranger from Craigslist to slap him—no, really—*slap him*—every time he looked at Facebook during work hours. The next report he pulled from RescueTime showed that his productivity had shot up to 98 percent.

RescueTime may be a better option than WorkTime because of the free version as well as the extended options when you upgrade to Pro ($6/month)—plus, it's a lot prettier. You still get the same statistics of every last thing you do on the computer; and the upgrade lets you block distracting sites, pats you on the back when you've been working hard and tracks work on individual documents.

If you're looking for a system for a team, RescueTime prices start at $30/month for two users. The site makes it clear that the system won't secretly monitor employee usage. Instead, it promises to increase productivity by helping your employees analyze their own work habits and cut out time-wasting behaviors.

For a quick fix, you can try simple site blockers. Visit **KeepMeOut.com** and enter a URL of a site you tend to frequent too frequently. Then you tell it how often you should be allowed to check back in. KeepMeOut creates a URL that you can bookmark in your browser. Click on the bookmark, and it lets you through, but the clock starts ticking. When you go back before you're supposed to, KeepMeOut wags its finger.

LeechBlock is another tool designed to block those time-wasting sites that can suck the life out of your working day. All you need to do is specify which sites to block and when to block them. You can specify up to six sets of sites to block, with different times and days for each set. You can block sites within fixed time periods (e.g., from 9 a.m. to 5 p.m.), after a time limit (e.g., 10 minutes in every hour), or with a combination of time periods and time limit (e.g., 10 minutes in every hour from 9 a.m. to 5 p.m.). You can also set a password for access to the extension options, just to slow you down in moments of weakness!

Time Management at a Glance

(recommended tools in **bold**)

KeepMeOut	Free site that lets you lock yourself out of sites that distract	Free	keepmeout.com
LeechBlock	Browser add-on that helps you block sites that suck your productivity	Free	proginosko.com/ leechblock.html
RescueTime	Web-based automatic time tracker for Mac and PC	Pro version starts at $6 a month	rescuetime.com
WorkTime	**Windows-based automatic time-tracking program**	**One-time fee of $29.95 for home edition**	**nestersoft.com**

Automation Tools

iBeam.it

IFTTT

Wappwolf

Zapier

Without even realizing it, you probably do the same tasks over and over—such as checking the weather, saving attachments from emails, tweeting your latest blog post on Twitter.

Though it takes just a few minutes to complete each task, these little jobs add up fast, and you probably have better uses of your time in today's crazy-busy lifestyle.

IFTTT, which stands for "if this, then that," is one of a category of tools that will help you automate some of these little tasks so you don't have to think about them. After you sign up for an account on IFTTT, link your cloud services, such as Dropbox, Twitter, Gmail and YouTube. Then set up recipes for actions, such as, "If someone tags a picture of me on Facebook, save it in Evernote" or "Send me a text message if it looks like rain."

Wappwolf is another type of automator, but it focuses on three major cloud services: Dropbox, Google Drive and Box. Wappwolf will let you create a rule like "Every time I put a document into a certain Dropbox folder, convert it to a PDF." It has some really cool picture-editing automations, such as the capability to add text to any image added to a Dropbox folder. Wappwolf also offers cross-platform automation with **iBeam.it**, which lets you save something with your favorite tool but offers triggers so your followers can use their preferred formats (e.g., You upload something to Dropbox, and your followers can choose to have it pop into their Flickr account).

Another automation tool, **Zapier,** offers the widest variety of channels; but I don't like the pricing structure. The free version limits the channels you can use as well as the number of recipes and the number of times they are activated, and the first paid plan is a pricy $15/month and still has plenty of limitations. IFTTT is 100 percent free. Wappwolf has strange pricing: It's mostly free for most of the automations you might need, but upgrading is—get this—$5 for a week or $5 for a month, downgradable at any time.

Customer-Service Tools

Get Human

Lucyphone

TalkTo

A 2012 survey found that more than half of us spend 10 to 20 minutes on hold every week, which adds up to 13 hours a year and 43 days in a lifetime. How irritating is that? You can save time and sanity by using a service that will sit on hold for you. Just search for the company you'd like to contact using the **Lucyphone** apps or website, and the site will call it for you and then give you a call when Lucyphone finally gets a human on the line.

You can also visit the very helpful **GetHuman** site, which lists the phone numbers and secret pathways to a live operator. GetHuman also works with Lucyphone for the callback service, plus it connects you directly with live chat systems and offers the best email address for getting results.

TalkTo is an almost unnerving site. You can find any business—and I mean any business, even my old freelance writing biz was listed—

and send a text or online question. Somehow, some way, TalkTo finds someone to answer your question. Then you can get the response via email, text or online. TalkTo operators act as conduits; and it's a little strange because the TalkTo rep—not the company—will respond, but they do it in first person as if the company were talking directly to you. Still, it's an amazing way to find out if your local bakery has red velvet cupcakes without picking up the phone.

Automation and Customer-Service Tools at a Glance

(recommended tools in **bold**)

GetHuman	**Site and mobile apps that reveal shortcuts to contact real people at any company**	**Free**	**gethuman.com**
iBeam.it	Cross-platform automator to share content with followers	Free	ibeam.it
IFTTT	**Free multi-application automator for cloud services**	**Free**	**ifttt.com**
Lucyphone	Virtual queue website and app that stays on hold for you	Free	lucyphone.com
TalkTo	**Site and apps that facilitate contact with any company through text and email**	**Free**	**talkto.com**
Wappwolf	Automation tool for Google Drive, Dropbox and Box	Free for most automations, or starting at $5/month for premium subscription	wappwolf.com
Zapier	Multi-application automator with more than 200 channels	Free for Standard Level with limits on channels and automations, or starting at $15/month	zapier.com

Behind the Glasses:
Playing With Crazy Tech Names

IFTTT is supposed to rhyme with "lift," but I can't help but pronounce it IF-Tuh-Tuh-Tuh. And there is a project management tool called Scrumy that sounds like "drummy," but I look at it and see "Screw-Me." Plus you can't help but laugh at a company called DimDim (which was purchased by Salesforce, Page 140, and shut down), whose employees told me they locked themselves in a room and brainstormed names for hours. DimDim was the best they could come up with?

And Wappwolf? Really? Even the tool owners made fun of its name on the site for their new product, iBeam.it.

> **Why introducing a new brand iBeam.it?**
>
> *Wepwuff? Wopwulf? Who ever knew how to spell Wappwolf correctly right from the start?*
>
> *Any more questions?*

These crazy tech names crack me up, make me shake my head or compel me to mispronounce them. Maybe they are all spending too much time generating domain and tech company names on sites like dotomator.com, which provides hours of brainstorming fun.

Chapter 8

Email and Information Management Tools

In this chapter:

I probably don't have to tell you these statistics because you're probably living them. According to the McKinsey Global Institute, workers spend about 28 percent of each day on email (2012 study). Another report by Experian Marketing Services showed a sharp increase in email access via mobile devices (78 percent in the United States); and after talking and texting, we're checking and answering email on our devices more than other activities.

And another nonsurprising fact about email: We're drowning in it. A statistic I read says we send or receive more than 100 emails a day. That's a lot of messaging, and that's just email.

In 2012, a group called DOMO released an infographic that claimed that every minute online:

✔ WordPress users write 347 new blog posts.

✔ YouTube users add 48 hours of video.

✔ Tweeters send 100,000 tweets.

And other statistics say that there are kabillions of deca-terabytes of data uploaded every nanosecond. OK, perhaps I'm exaggerating; but I do know that if it weren't for awesome tools such as the ones in this chapter, we would be buried in information with no way to get organized.

It's no wonder that email and information tools are a fast-growing area of technology, with apps and tools popping up daily to help us manage information overload.

Email Volume Control

| HitMeLater |
| NutshellMail |
| Unroll.me |

How many newsletters do you get a week? How about all those listserv messages from your association? Or the notifications from Twitter that you have a new follower? All these emails can clog up your inbox and keep you from getting to the messages you actually need to read.

Many of the tools that help you manage your subscriptions in bulk are attached to Gmail or other web-based email systems. For Gmail, I have used **Unroll.me**. You just give Unroll.me permission to search your Gmail inbox, and all your subscriptions show up, giving you the option to unsubscribe, unsubscribe and delete all messages, or receive in a daily digest.

For managing social network notifications and updates, I recommend **NutshellMail** from Constant Contact. Connect your social media accounts through the site, and you can choose to receive digests in your inbox with all the updates you desire. And you can reply to any tweets or posts through NutshellMail directly without having to go to each site.

When you can't respond to an email right away, just forward it to 24@hitmelater.com, and **HitMeLater** will resend it to you 24 hours later. Or send it to yourself in four hours with 4@hitmelater.com or next week with Tuesday@hitmelater.com.

Email and Contact Management

Mailbox
Rapportive
Smartr
Xobni
Yesware

If I have to name the PC-only feature that I was most sad to leave when I switched to Mac, I'd have to say it's **Xobni**.

Xobni, which is "inbox" spelled backward, is a plug-in for Microsoft Outlook that completely transformed how I worked with my email. Once you install Xobni, your Xobni dashboard appears in your inbox. When you get an email, you see all kinds of critical information about your contact, including every single email you've exchanged, every person who has been included in your email threads, every attachment you've shared. Amazing stuff. You can also see statistics that can help improve your communication techniques, such as the times of the day that your contact usually sends emails.

Another level of awesomeness is its integration into LinkedIn. You can see if your contacts are connected to LinkedIn; and if you're not connected yet, Xobni offers a button to let you write a personal note with an invitation to connect. Xobni also has integrations with Evernote, Facebook and Salesforce.

There are plenty of other little tricks, but my favorite feature is a simple one. How many times have you gotten an email about a meeting and had to switch to your calendar to check availability? You have to switch back and forth between the inbox and the calendar, cutting and pasting phone numbers, figuring out meeting times. But when you have Xobni, the program shows the last email you viewed in the dashboard. No more flipping back and forth.

The Xobni product itself is only available for Microsoft Outlook for Windows, which is why I had to give it up. Sniff. But the company also produces a contact manager called **Smartr** (which is similar to another tool,

Rapportive), available for Gmail as well as Android, iOS and BlackBerry devices.

If you use Gmail for business, you will love **Yesware.** It's a simple add-on to your web-based Gmail inbox (Chrome and Firefox browsers) that allows you to track when people open your email. It may sound a little cyber-stalker-ish, but in practice it's handy to make sure your proposal was received or your email server didn't get flagged for spam again. I also appreciate the capability to create quick templates for common responses so you don't have to retype the same "Thank you for writing" email a dozen times a month.

A study by Experian in May of 2013 revealed that we spend about an hour on our smartphones every day, with email being the most-used feature besides texting and talking; and the **Mailbox** app can make that time more efficient. Mailbox loads your email messages into list format then helps you sort with a swipe into piles, such as delete, save or remind me later. My biggest pet peeve is that it's easy to misswipe, and shaking to undo that action requires one heck of a shake.

NerdHerd Favorite: Letter Opener

Microsoft and Apple don't always play well together, especially when it comes to their proprietary email readers. When Outlook smashes its attachments and appointments into a winmail.dat file, Judy Kaban uses **Letter Opener** to seamlessly convert the file into its original format. "Letter Opener saves a lot of frustration."

Email Management at a Glance

(recommended tools in **bold**)

Gmail	**Email aggregator that gives you access from anywhere**	**Free**	**gmail.com**
HitMeLater	Scheduling emails	Free to schedule under 24 hours, or within the month or year starts at $12/year	hitmelater.com
Letter Opener	Mac download and iOS app that converts Outlook winmail.dat files into original attachments and appointments	Free for app, or $6.99 for Lite version for Mac	creativeinaustralia.com/letteropenerlite
Mailbox	Inbox zero helper for Gmail and iOS	Coming soon	mailboxapp.com
NutshellMail	Constant Contact service to manage social media notifications	Free	nutshellmail.com
Rapportive	LinkedIn-owned contact and email manager for Gmail	Free	rapportive.com
Smartr	Contact and email manager for mobile devices and Gmail	Free	xobni.com
Unroll.me	Email subscription manager for Gmail and Yahoo	Free	unroll.me
Xobni	**Contact and email manager for Microsoft Outlook for Windows**	**Free, or $47.95/ year for Pro**	**xobni.com**
Yesware	**Gmail tool to track emails and manage templates**	**Free for up to 100 tracked emails a month, or starting at $5/month for pro features**	yesware.com

Behind the Glasses: Why I Love Gmail

Gmail has become my email management of choice for all five of my email addresses. You can import all your email accounts into your Gmail inbox and automatically apply a label as they come in. Gmail has a number of add-ons that can help you sort and track them, plus you can access all your accounts everywhere you can access your Gmail.

Oh, and it's free, of course.

My Gmail helpers:

- ✔ Gmail apps on all iOS devices, including my present favorite, Mailbox app

- ✔ Yesware (Page 101) for email and lead tracking plus templates ($5/month)

- ✔ Smartr (Page 100) for contact management

- ✔ Attachments.me to insert and download Dropbox documents from the cloud

- ✔ Multiple Inboxes feature from Gmail Labs to divide up my email accounts on the page

- ✔ Multiple signatures set up for different email addresses

- ✔ Zopim (Page 50) notifications through chat for visitors to our sites

Note Taking and Organization

Evernote

LectureNotes

LectureRecordings

Notability

Onenote

I'll go out on a very safe limb here and say that **Evernote** is the king of note-taking and information organization apps. Since its release in 2008, it has grown exponentially and ubiquitously, gaining millions of loyal followers and creating integrations into dozens and dozens of other apps and programs.

In a nutshell, Evernote is the thick pile of manila folders that sits on the corner of your desk with all the projects you're working on. These are the folders that have the paperclips, scraps of paper, sticky notes and handwritten notes all related to your important projects.

Evernote is that folder in digital format, available anywhere and everywhere, instantly synchronized and easily shared. You can store pictures, documents, notes, webpages, snippets of text, handwritten napkins, emails and anything else you can possibly imagine. The search engine even combs text in pictures (and in PDFs for Premium subscribers).

You can add your information to Evernote in every possible way as well—through browser plug-ins, email, web apps, desktop apps and mobile apps. When you have the information you want, you can tag it, organize it into folders, share it and search for it. Evernote competes directly with Microsoft's **OneNote**, which costs about $80 if you buy it alone, or free if you use the web app.

To replicate the nostalgic feeling of taking notes with pen and paper, a couple of tablet apps can help. The **Notability** iPad app combines handwritten or typed notes with audio recordings to help you truly capture the ideas of a meeting or brainstorming session. It synchronizes with

Dropbox to save your notes for access anywhere. For Android tablets, you might try **LectureNotes** in conjunction with **LectureRecordings** to sync notes and audio and export to Evernote. Both handwriting apps are helpful for marking up PDFs and other documents as well.

Content Aggregators

Feedly

Flipboard

Instapaper

Pocket

The Old Reader

In 2012, **Flipboard** made my list of the top three most influential tools in my toolbox because it's a resource I use every single day. Flipboard can import all your RSS feeds plus give you access to amazing, customized content—all in a clever, attractive magazine format.

Another popular feed reader, **Feedly,** boasted that more than 3 million Google Reader users switched to its service when Reader died in 2013. The service was already taking off; and when Google Reader announced the end, the numbers went through the roof. I don't much like the name of another service because it seems, well, old. But if you miss the old Google Reader, **The Old Reader** is for you. It's a pure RSS feed with social sharing.

Pocket allows you to tuck any article or website into a virtual folder to read later from anywhere: your Nook, Android devices, iOS devices, desktops or other devices. You'll find options to save to Pocket on many major sites and readers, allowing you to instantly add articles and pages to your account to read anywhere. Pocket is free. **Instapaper** is a lot like Pocket. Prices vary by app, and you can upgrade to a subscription service for a buck a month.

Sticky Notes

7 Sticky Notes

Yellow

If you're still stuck on your sticky note system, check out **7 Sticky Notes** for Windows or **Yellow** for Macs. They give you the cool look and functionality of our favorite little gummy notepads, and you can add them all over your desktop without killing any trees.

Research Tools

Mendeley

Zotero

Boy, do kids today have it easy (insert old lady sigh).

The first time I wrote a paper that required footnotes and a bibliography, I had to type it on a typewriter and count the number of lines to leave at the bottom to leave space for the notes. And about a decade after that when I wrote my master's thesis, I kept track of my bibliography on handwritten index cards.

Zotero and **Mendeley** can take a good deal of the pain out of maintaining a bibliography and tracking citations in any scholarly report. With Zotero, you simply need to download the browser add-on (Firefox is the main one.) to grab citations straight from the web. You can also add references manually through the add-on or using the stand-alone desktop tool.

Adding a citation or creating a bibliography with Zotero is even easier. Just choose a citation style (Chicago or APA or others) then press a button or two. Your source is inserted without error.

Mendeley gives you similar downloadables plus 1GB of storage for free and also offers access via your iOS devices.

Information Tools at a Glance

(recommended tools in **bold**)

7 Sticky Notes	Windows-based sticky notes	Free	7stickynotes.com
Evernote	**Note-taking and information organizing app for every device**	**Free for most features, or $45/ year for Premium**	**evernote.com**
Feedly	RSS feed reader	Free	feedly.com
Flipboard	**Content aggregation and delivery app**	**Free**	**flipboard.com**
Instapaper	Tool to save articles and information to read later on any device	Free for browser bookmarklets, or various prices for apps	instapaper.com
LectureNotes	Android note-taking app	$4.33	In the Google play store
LectureRecordings	Android audio-recording app used with LectureNotes	$1.34	In the Google play store
Mendeley	Free bibliography and reference tool for Word and OpenOffice with iOS apps	Free for up to 1GB of storage, or starting at $4.99/month for premium services	mendeley.com
Notability	**Note-taking iPad app with audio recording functionality**	**$1.99**	**gingerlabs.com/ cont/notability.php**
OneNote	Note-taking and information organizing tool	Free with Office Web Apps and related mobile apps	office.microsoft.com/ en-us/web-apps
Pocket	Tool to save articles and information to read later on any device	Free	getpocket.com

Information Tools at a Glance (continued)

The Old Reader	Simple Google Reader-like RSS feed	Free	theoldreader.com
Yellow	Mac-based sticky notes	Free	yellow-app.com
Zotero	Free bibliography and reference tool for Word and LibreOffice	Free for software downloads and up to 100MB online storage, or starting at $5/month for more storage	zotero.org

This book is interactive!
Scan with the Layar App for
updates, bonus material and more

Chapter 9

Personal Tools

Think of this section as your starting point for New Year's Resolutions. These tools and tips will help you set goals, get a job, protect your reputation and get things done.

Right before I graduated from college in 1990, I bought a giant box of 100 percent cotton bond resumé paper, carefully photocopied clips of my best newspaper articles and handwrote addresses on 30+ envelopes to newspapers all over the country that might hire me.

Our career counselors back then pointed out that our resumés and clip portfolios were the only resources that these hiring managers would ever have to figure out who we are and what we could offer. What a different world we live in now! If you apply for a job, you're likely to do it online; and the hiring manager can Google you in seconds to see your online portfolio, view your professional connections, or, unfortunately, see where you partied graduation night.

We have tools today that help us maximize the power of technology to showcase your best side, as well as resources that help you manage your reputation.

Resumé and Portfolio Tools

LinkedIn
Resumé Builder

re.vu

ResumUP

I've long maintained that LinkedIn is the single most powerful job search tool out there, so it makes sense that it would help you create a resume. The **Resumé Builder** is hidden in the LinkedIn Labs. Simply log in to LinkedIn from the resume site, and your information is instantly transformed into an attractive resumé format. Choose your favorite template, then simply download as a PDF.

The site looks pretty abandoned by LinkedIn, which ordinarily would cause me to skip it. But it's still handy for a quick, professional resumé.

If you're looking for something a little bit snazzier, **re.vu** is another site that pulls your LinkedIn profile to tell a visual story of your work history, complete with infographics, uploads and all kinds of cool graphics. You can also upload files, including a downloadable resume in a more traditional format. Even if you're not job searching, it's a great place to pull together an attractive, professional snapshot of who you are and what you've done. **ResumUP** has some cool features as well. Both of these sites are free (for now).

Reputation Managers

AccountKiller

BrandYourself

Google Alerts

If you are a professional, you need to be using **Google Alerts.** With Google Alerts, you can track keywords in the web world in news articles, blogs and other citations. Set them up for your company's name, your name, even hot keywords in your field. You will receive emails that list places your alerts were mentioned on the web.

I set them up for my last name, my company and keywords related to my clients. Every mention is aggregated and delivered via email. This saves me the hassle of doing "ego searches."

If your front-page Google results are less than desirable, **BrandYourself** can help. You can sign up for free monitoring and submit good sites (like your LinkedIn profile) so that your search results look more professional and are truly yours (not another Beth Ziesenis).

Another way to do damage control is to close public (or private) profiles you may have lingering on sites you no longer use. How many site subscriptions do you have? Facebook, Yahoo, Skype, Groupon—maybe even an old Myspace account? **AccountKiller** lists hundreds of popular signup sites and rates them white, gray or black for how easy it is to unsubscribe to them, plus gives you pointers on removing your personal information. *Warning: Some of the sites it lists are not safe for work.*

Security Check: Self-Destructing Emails and Pictures

Ever share a picture that you hope your parents will never see? Teenagers have fallen in love with **Snapchat,** an app that sends pictures that will self-destruct. That way you and your friends can share a laugh, but your mom will never know.

Just like the self-destructing pictures in Snapchat, **Burn Note** creates a self-destructing, private email thread that has safeguards against copying or even screenshots. These kinds of services are great keeping things secret from normal computer users, but remember that *nothing really disappears* from the web.

Job and Reputation Tools at a Glance (recommended tools in **bold**)

AccountKiller	Directory of public profile sites with instructions on how to delete accounts	Free	accountkiller.com
BrandYourself	**Reputation service that helps enhance Google searches for your name and business**	**Free for many features, or $9.99/month for more**	**brandyourself.com**
Burn Note	Self-destructing, copy-resistant messages	Free	burnnote.com
Google Alerts	**Google tool that sends emails when keywords appear in searches**	**Free**	**google.com/alerts**
LinkedIn Resumé Builder	Instant resumés from LinkedIn profiles	Free	resume.linkedinlabs.com
re.vu	**Resumé pages and sites**	**Free**	**re.vu**
ResumUP	Instant visual resumé builder	Free	resumup.com
Snapchat	Mobile app that sends self-destructing pictures	Free	snapchat.com

Goal-Setting Tools

21habit

GymPact

Juice

Sleep Time

stickK

Unstuck

Many of the goal-setting tools out there add a little weight to your motivation by tying money into the equation. We've heard experts say that it takes 21 days to make or break a habit. That's the basis of the site called **21habit,** a simple tool that helps you describe a habit then asks you to check in daily to record your progress in making or breaking it.

You can simply track your habit progress, or you can pledge a certain amount to ensure your success. Meet your goal, and you get your money back. Miss a few days, and your money goes to a charity you designate.

GymPact makes you put your money where your muscles are. You make a monetary commitment to work out a certain number of times a week, and the GymPact apps help you track them. If you make your weekly goal, you earn money. Miss it, and you pay into the communal pool that pays the dedicated workout buddies.

Another way to meet a goal is to make it public and find people to keep you accountable. A free site called **stickK** lets you set your goals and pledge a private monetary commitment to your chosen "referee." Your referee has the last call on whether you met your goal; and if not, he gets the money.

It's unfortunate that **Unstuck** is available only on iPads because this is a resource we can all use. Although it's not tied to money like the other goal-setting tools, Unstuck has a beautiful interface that takes you through a series of questions to identify and work through challenges in your life that leave you "stuck."

There are no shortages of health-monitoring apps to help you find a better work/life balance, but I do like a couple in particular. The little **Juice** app helps you discover the keys to more energy by making it easy for you to track mood, energy level, nutrition and sleep patterns. The interface is adorable; and tracking takes just a few clicks a day, so it's easy to use.

Perhaps it's just because I find nerdy comfort in sleeping with my iPhone, but I also like **Sleep Time** on the road. Sleep Time monitors your tossing and turning to analyze your sleep cycles, then it wakes you in a light sleep window so you feel more refreshed.

Goal-Setting Tools at a Glance (recommended tools in **bold**)

21habit	Goal-setting site that helps you make or break a habit in 21 days	Free for basic, or $21 for Committed Mode	21habit.com
GymPact	**Mobile app to track workouts for accountability**	**Free for app, and flexible pricing for goal commitment**	**gym-pact.com**
Juice	**iOS app to track mood, energy, nutrition**	**Free**	**mindbloom.com/ juice**
Sleep Time	Mobile alarm clock that monitors sleep patterns	Free and paid versions	azumio.com/apps/ sleep-time
stickK	Goal-setting site with financial commitment and accountability partner	Free for service, with financial commitments of your choosing	stickk.com
Unstuck	**iPad app that helps you identify and remove personal roadblocks**	**Free**	**unstuck.com**

NerdHerd Favorite: Everything iOS

Debbi Haddaway is a nerd after my own heart. She says her favorite tools are Apple apps—everything! "I love all techy, nerdy stuff!" she says.

Brainstorming Tools

Bubbl.us

FreeMind

iThoughts

RhymeZone

SimpleMind

SpiderScribe

Visual Thesaurus

No matter how many other mind-mapping tools I come across, for a quick brainstorming session, I keep returning to the cute and free **Bubbl.us** app. It's easy to use and fun to play with. Another simple site, **SpiderScribe,** allows you to add text, images, files and events, plus you can embed the creations into your site.

FreeMind is a reader favorite, a free mind-mapping application written in Java. (The jury is still out on whether Java is safe.) FreeMind encompasses a fine range of features, including scads of icons and color formatting options to help you visually organize concepts. It also supports hyperlinks, which allow you to link websites and even documents to a map. In addition, you'll be able to export your landscape of thoughts in a variety of formats, including HTML, PDF and JPEG. As flexible as it lets your mind be, FreeMind works within an older-style logical structure that could get frustrating for some. For instance, you must insert nodes by hand or using a hot key; you can't click and drag to create them (a shame).

On iOS devices, try the **iThoughts** apps, which let you create mind maps that can be exported to other systems. If you're looking for a unified system, you might try the **SimpleMind** tools, which you can purchase on iOS and Android devices as well as PCs and Macs. You can buy the apps for different platforms and synchronize across all devices.

Sometimes you need inspiration from ideas, words and concepts. You'll spend way too much time playing around on **Visual Thesaurus,** and before you know it, it'll be warning you that your trial is up. You put in your word, and an interactive spider web-type graphic explodes on the screen with a range of word choices. It's a great place to brainstorm, learn and play. Or try **RhymeZone** to find rhyming words, antonyms, synonyms and homonyms.

Brainstorming and Word Tools at a Glance

(recommended tools in **bold**)

Bubbl.us	**Online mind-mapping tool**	**Free**	**bubbl.us**
FreeMind	Open-source downloadable mind-mapping program	Free	freemind.sourceforge.net
iThoughts	iOS mind-mapping app	Price varies, less than $10	ithoughts.co.uk
RhymeZone	Simple site for finding words that rhyme	Free	rhymezone.com
SimpleMind	Desktop and mobile mind-mapping apps	Ranging from free versions of mobile apps to bundles for PCs and Macs	simpleapps.eu/simplemind
SpiderScribe	Online mind-mapping software	Free for personal use, or pro levels start at $5/month	spiderscribe.net
Visual Thesaurus	**Word-exploring website for synonyms, antonyms and brainstorming**	**Free for a very brief trial, or $2.95/month for full version**	**visualthesaurus.com**

NerdHerd Favorite: KidGlyphs

This tool doesn't really fit into other sections of the book, but it's worth a share. When I was freelancing, I had the pleasure of writing for DrGreene.com and Cheryl Greene. Cheryl and team have developed **KidGlyphs**, an app that teaches toddlers to communicate. Cheryl says, "This simple tool helps toddlers learn to communicate faster and can play a role in easing 'the terrible twos.'"

Work Environment Tools

DarkCopy
Ergonomics Simplified
f.lux
FocusWriter
iA Writer
Readability

Shhhh, be very, very quiet. I'm trying to work!

If you're as old as I am, you'll remember the computers of days gone by, where you had a black screen and a blinking green cursor box. You didn't have to check email every 10 minutes because there was no real email as we know it. No Facebook, no Twitter, no nuthin'—just you and a blank screen.

DarkCopy brings you back to those days with a simple, elegant tool to help you blot out all the intoxicating distractions of today's busy world. Just visit the site, expand the black screen to full size, and you're transported back to pre-Windows 3.1. There are absolutely no bells or whistles, and that's what makes it great. Just don't get so Zen that you forget to copy and paste your text into your own document.

Other favorite tools are **iA Writer** for Mac and iOS devices and **FocusWriter,** an unfancy download for Mac and PC. You may also find some distraction-free tools built into your word-processing software, such as Microsoft Word's Focus View option for working in a document.

Readability is a different type of clutter-reduction tool. Web pages have pictures, pop-ups, ads and other floaties that can make it hard to quickly scan an interesting article to get the facts. Readability can help in a couple of different ways. Its original purpose was to strip the extraneous distractions from an article so you can actually read the text. It still does that in browsers and on mobile devices, but now it does more.

With the new generation of Readability, you can read the article now with zero distractions or save it into a folder to read later. You can also send it to your Kindle (the device or even a free software download) to read at your convenience.

You can't get much done if you're uncomfortable at your desk. The quiz on **Ergonomics Simplified** takes you through a series of questions about your chair position, your mouse and your monitor height. Although I ran across a few questions that didn't have answers that applied, I learned much about proper monitor height, mouse adjustment, seat specifics and footrests. The evaluation gives you tips as you answer the questions, and at the end you get a full list of problem areas and recommendations for products (which it sells). But the free quiz is well worth a few minutes.

My former assistant Claire Parrish stumbled upon this tool: **f.lux** adapts the lighting level of your computer's display to the time of day. e.g., warm at night and like sunlight during the day. f.lux makes your computer screen look like the room you're in, all the time. When the sun sets, it makes your computer look like your indoor lights. In the morning, it makes your screen look like sunlight again.

NerdHerd Favorites: Clearly and OmmWriter

Olivia Resch likes DarkCopy, but she loves **OmmWriter**, which plays soft music and has a calming background so you can gather your thoughts and be creative on your Mac, PC or iPad. And Michele Huber is in love with Evernote's **Clearly** browser plugin for Chrome and Firefox because "it takes away clutter and unimportant information from a webpage." Clearly also lets you save articles and more directly into your Evernote account.

Work Environment Tools at a Glance (recommended tools in **bold**)

Clearly	Evernote browser plugin that removes ads and other distractions from webpages	Free	evernote.com/clearly
DarkCopy	**Simple, full-screen online text editor for distraction-free writing**	**Free**	**darkcopy.com**
Ergonomics Simplified	**Free questionnaire to evaluate office ergonomics**	**Free**	**ergonomicssimplified.com**
f.lux	Downloadable program that adjusts the lighting of your PC, Mac or iOS device	Free	stereopsis.com/flux
FocusWriter	Plain Jane word processor download to help you focus	Free	gottcode.org/focuswriter
iA Writer	**Simple word processor for Mac and iOS devices**	**App prices vary, but less than $10**	**iawriter.com**
OmmWriter	Distraction-free word processor with soft music and graphics for increased productivity (Mac, PC, iPad)	Free for basic, or $4.99 for iPad app or upgrade	ommwriter.com
Readability	**Browser plug-in and app that strips ads and clutter from the web**	**Free**	**readability.com**

Chapter 10

Personal and Business Financial Tools

In this chapter:

I put off writing this chapter until the very end for one reason:

I hate money.

That's crazy, right? How can someone hate money? I'm not sure what happened in my childhood that turned me off dollar signs, numbers and figures; but I avoid them whenever I can. Accounting discussions make my nose crinkle up. Expense reports make my belly hurt. And I'd rather eat a liver-flavor cupcake with pickle frosting than reconcile a bank statement. I even hate going to the bank and will contentiously avoid a check on the table until I accidentally use it as a coaster.

Luckily my husband *really* likes money and almost chose a career in accounting over becoming a lawyer. He leaves me alone to joyously pursue my goal of making people happy by sharing free tools, and that's the way I want it.

My dislike of dollar signs aside, my husband and I have worked out financial solutions for our business; and in the process I've learned plenty about the different systems available to small businesses.

Payment Tools

GoPayment
LevelUp
PayPal Here
Square
Square Wallet

In the past year, **Square** has expanded at a disappointing speed. By disappointing, I mean an amazing speed, infiltrating businesses everywhere. That's disappointing because I started using Square when it was unknown, and I'm a little sad it's not my super secret weapon anymore.

Square changed business payment systems overnight. Before it took off, small businesses had to mess with point-of-sale terminal rentals, variable (and mysterious) credit card processing fees, long contracts and the irritation of receipt paper that jammed in the machine. Square invented a little gadget that fits into a mobile device's audio jack to create an instant pay station. It charges 2.75 percent for every swipe; and there are no other fees, obligations or hassles. The money appears into your bank account within a day or two. The tablet versions let you set up a cash register-type interface, which looks as cool as it works.

Square is also changing the way you interact with customers. **Square Wallet** is its consumer app that lets customers pay for products just by saying their names at the register. Weird, right? Here's how it works: when a customer has Square Wallet, he can locate a business that works with Square on his app. Then he can push a button to enable a hands-free payment; and when he approaches the register, the employee will see the customer's picture on the Square Register. And if someone goes to the same Starbucks every day, he can set up the store as a permanent hands-free location. Then it's kind of like Norm walking into *Cheers*. (If you were born after 1993, you may miss this reference.)

PayPal and Intuit have both jumped into the mobile payment water after Square. **PayPal Here's** fees are slightly lower, and your money goes straight into your PayPal account instead of your bank account. If you use Quick-Books (See why I don't, Page 132.), **GoPayment** integrates into your account to help you track sales. GoPayment has similar transaction fees to the other two, plus a nice level if you process more than $1,500/month: a $12.95/month fee plus a lower per-swipe rate of 1.7 percent.

All three services have free mobile readers and apps for Android and iOS devices, and you can expect to pay 1 percent plus more for manual transactions vs. card swipes.

While Square, PayPal Here and GoPayment are best known for functionality on the business side, **LevelUp** is popular mainly for its convenience (and fun) for consumers.

LevelUp is another mobile payment app. Businesses sign up for LevelUp for free, and they are listed in the directory. When the office party guy shouts, "It's 5 o'clock somewhere!" and prompts the staff into a happy hour outing, he can use LevelUp to locate deals at bars in the area. When he picks up the first round of drinks with the app, he earns rewards in the form of credits he can spend at other LevelUp businesses. Square Wallet is creeping into this space, but LevelUp's reward system is addicting for consumers. On the business side, LevelUp charges a flat 2 percent to process the transactions; or you can sign up for its advertising campaigns, where it promotes you but takes 40 percent of the money if customers take advantage of the deal (kind of like a Groupon).

Payment Tools at a Glance

(recommended tools in **bold**)

GoPayment	Intuit's mobile payment system	2.7% for swiped transactions, or 1.7% with a monthly subscription of $12.95	gopayment.com
LevelUp	**Mobile payment app with integrated advertising**	**2%/transaction**	**levelup.com**
PayPal Here	PayPal's mobile payment system	2.7%/swipe	paypal.com/webapps/ mpp/credit-card-reader
Square	**Mobile payment system for consumers and businesses**	**2.75%/swipe, or $275/month with no processing fees**	**squareup.com**
Square Wallet	Consumer mobile payment system	Free	squareup.com/wallet

Expense Management Tools

Concur

Expensify

Lemon Wallet

OneReceipt

Shoeboxed

Wave Accounting

Xpenser

OK, 'fess up. Do you have a pile of wrinkled, stained, faded receipts sitting around your office that you're supposed to do something with? It's time to take control with these receipt management tools.

All things considered, my favorite receipt management tool is still **Shoeboxed**, even though there are less expensive alternatives out there. Shoeboxed will process your electronic and paper receipts and other documents, starting at about $10/month for up to 50 scans. There's no feeling more wonderful than stuffing an envelope with all those random receipts and shipping them off to North Carolina to be someone else's problem. Shoeboxed's technology reads the receipts, categorizes them, adds them up, lets you tag them and can merge them together into a super-tidy expense report that will make any accountant happy.

Expensify and **Xpenser** are my other favorites in this category. Both let you snap pictures of your receipts on the go, just like Shoeboxed, but they both go further in giving you a full financial picture by integrating credit card and bank statements. Xpenser has a cool feature that lets you text, call or tweet in your expenses, though you don't get much unless you pay $9 a month. Expensify also gives you all kinds of ways of managing your receipts, including synchronizing through Evernote. It will analyze your receipt via SmartScan 10 times a month for free, and then it's 20 cents/scan.

If I had been smart, instead of upgrading to TripIt Pro (Page 239) for $50 a year, I would have purchased the $8/month **Concur** system, which includes and integrates with TripIt Pro, letting you associate expenses with different trips.

Concur is used by a lot of large companies to allow employees to track expenses on the go and make expense reports easier. The main drawback is that when you snap a receipt on your mobile device, you still have to enter the data manually, although the system will attach the receipt to your expense report.

Wave Accounting, my favorite accounting tool (Page 130), is venturing into the receipts area with an iOS app that snaps and analyzes receipts. **OneReceipt** has promise. It's still in beta and free, but it looks like it'll be a useful manager for receipts.

I might also give **Lemon Wallet** a try, though in 2013 it discontinued its free receipt analysis service. Lemon Wallet specializes in keeping track of all your plastic. You can enter all your cards into the app, allowing you to use your credit cards on the go and giving you a backup in case you lose a card. It's free for the basic service, but advanced features such as personal assistance to cancel cards if you lose your wallet come with the paid levels.

This book is interactive!
Scan with the Layar App for
updates, bonus material and more

Expense Management Tools at a Glance

(recommended tools in **bold**)

Concur	Expense and travel manager (integrated with TripIt)	Starting at $8/month	concur.com
Expensify	Expense report manager and tracker	Robust free version, or $5-$10/user/month for company expense report management	expensify.com
Lemon Wallet	Financial card organization and management tool with receipt tracking	Free for basic, or starting at $39.99/year for extras such as lost wallet assistance	lemon.com
OneReceipt	**Electronic receipt management for iOS and online**	**Free**	**onereceipt.com**
Shoeboxed	**Digital and hard-copy expense manager**	**Free for basic plan for electronic receipts, or paid with hard-copy scans startsat $9.95/month**	**shoeboxed.com**
Xpenser	Expense management system that takes receipts via phone, text, email and Twitter	Free plan for up to 300 receipts, or full-service starting at $9/user/month	xpenser.com

Money Management Tools

Mint
SigFig
Simple

Mint has been around since 2005, and it's the top budget management tool for individuals that sets the standard for other services in this category. I'm at a loss to think of a reason you wouldn't go with Mint for your budgeting. Gather all your financial information into one area, then set up an account on Mint.com to start tracking your expenses and managing your budget. The system takes you a few minutes to set up, and then all of your expenses and income are in the same place.

Mint provides partner recommendations that could save you money, such as suggesting a credit card that has a lower interest rate or recommending a high-interest bearing savings account. If you take it up on its offer, Mint makes money. If not, you can still use its budgeting system for free.

It took some research before I discovered the name origin of another cool tool, **SigFig**—more evidence that I purposefully avoid talking about accounting and finance. The name comes from a common abbreviation of "significant figures," which sounds like it means "numbers that matter." Still, it's tough to get past the name—SigFig. Just strange.

SigFig is another tool that pulls your financial investments into one place, but its goal is to dig through your statements for hidden fees and ways you can make more money. Like Mint, SigFig is free, making money from brokers or services that might benefit when you switch your investment strategy or adviser. It promises, promises, promises that its recommendations are objective; so you don't have to be concerned that it's steering you toward a move that will make it money rather than one that will be the best for you.

I can't think of a modern bank that doesn't have a mobile app these days, but what if the only place your bank exists is on your mobile devices and online? We're talking no marble floors, pens on strings or cheap lollipops.

Chapter 10 ~ Personal and Business Financial Tools

Simple is not actually a bank, but you probably won't be able to tell the difference. You keep money in it, get money from it, see where you spend your money and do most of the things that you would do at your regular bank. It operates via mobile apps (iOS and Android) as well as the website but has no brick-and-mortar offices.

It's much cooler than a regular bank, in both its concept and personality. Instead of staying on hold or waiting in line to get help, you message it through the app. To deposit a check, you snap a picture. And you can access your money through a network of 50,000 fee-free ATMs. There's a whole bunch of info on the site about fees and how it doesn't have them like other banks do, but I don't really pay attention to financial institution fine print.

Perhaps the coolest thing about Simple is its Mint-i-ness. Like the awesome Mint system, Simple helps you budget your money and keep track of your finances. I spoke to a Simple fan who loves the capability to set financial goals through the app, such as saving for a vacation. You set your goal, and Simple will show you a Safe-to-Spend dashboard that keeps you on your budget and will warn you if you are about to miss your target.

Money Management Tools at a Glance (recommended tools in **bold**)

Mint	**Award-winning free budgeting and expense management tool**	**Free**	**mint.com**
SigFig	Investment and portfolio manager with fee reviews and advice	Free	sigfig.com
Simple	Virtual bank service with budgeting and money management tools	Free for an account, plus basic bank fees	simple.com

Accounting Tools

Freshbooks

Gnucash

Paymo

Wave Accounting

I'm puzzled by the anonymous awesomeness of **Wave Accounting.** How can no one know about this service? Its competitors charge money—in some cases lots of money—for the same types of features: financial institution account management (personal and business), invoicing, receipt management and budget snapshots. It offers payroll services as well for the simple (and cheap) price of $5/employee. And yet, I rarely run across anyone else who uses it.

Perhaps the challenge is its lack of integrations into other systems. You can import all your financial accounts into the system, but that's about where the integrations end.

One of the top online accounting systems out there, **FreshBooks,** has a whole page of add-ons for its system, including project management, time tracking, lead generation and email. But FreshBooks' free level caps at three clients, and you'll pay $19.95/month or more for the paid versions. Another attractive competitor, **Paymo,** has time tracking and project management built in. It's free for one user and just one invoice a month (really? wow), but the full-featured package is just $14.85/month for up to three employees.

I have no idea what double-entry accounting is; but if you need it, **Gnu-Cash** has it. This open-source (read "free") download works for small-business accounting needs, including expense tracking, budgeting, reconciliation and invoicing. In today's access-anywhere world, Gnu-Cash's desktop-based download seems a little limiting. Even if you use the related Android app (by a different developer), you still have to enter transactions on the go then upload them into your software instead of the instant synchronization that we're used to. But the open-source community around GnuCash does a great job of keeping the software updated and adding new features.

One cool thing about GnuCash is that, unlike many of the tools in this book, the software is available for almost every known operating system, including GNU/Linux, BSD, Solaris, Mac and Windows.

Accounting Tools at a Glance

(recommended tools in **bold**)

FreshBooks	Fastest way to track time and invoice your clients	Free for 3 clients, or starting at $19.95/month for paid plans	freshbooks.com
GnuCash	Open-source accounting download for multiple platforms with double-entry bookkeeping system	Free	gnucash.org
Paymo	Online accounting system with time tracking, project management and invoicing	Full-featured free level allows 1 invoice/month, or starting at $9.95/month for 2 users and 25 invoices	paymo.biz
Wave Accounting	**Free online accounting system with receipt management and invoicing**	**Free for most features; $5/employee/month for payroll**	**waveaccounting.com**

Behind the Glasses: No QuickBooks for Me

I should mention QuickBooks here as a major competitor, but I really don't want to. I hate, hate, hate QuickBooks. My husband is my chief financial officer, and he talked me into paying almost $200 for the pro version. I found it confusing to set up (Wave took me less than 10 minutes.), and it's inflexible when it comes to goofs. (Want to delete an invoice permanently so no one sees how bad you messed it up? Good luck!) I also had to jump through all kinds of crazy hoops to pull my bank accounts into the software.

The biggest problem I had with it was customizing the templates for my invoice. It's not an intuitive process, even for a nerd like me; and it kept crashing. What's more, there was some kind of ridiculous warning that I could personalize it x number of times before it would charge me extra money for the privilege. I can't verify that I read that right because I could never get back to that page.

My husband promised he'd work with our bookkeeper to create a template for me, and that made me even more frustrated. Bless their hearts—it's not their fault, but the logo they chose printed out fuzzy. And they had misspelled several words, including my last name! And the worst thing? Oh gosh, it's so hard to talk about this. The worst thing was that they chose Comic Sans as the font! How could an invoice with a fuzzy logo and the world's most hated font be mine? I ground my teeth for about an hour as I worked to fix these problems, but I never did create something that looked professional enough to come from Your Nerdy Best Friend.

If you're one of the millions of QuickBooks fans, I'm happy for you. But I hope I never have to use it again.

Guest Nerd:
Shopping Tools from Leslie Herberger

Coupon Sherpa

Ebates

RetailMeNot

ShopSavvy

Slice

One of the best ways to save money while shopping online is to use coupon codes, also known as promotion codes. While there are several sites to use, **RetailMeNot** is easy to use and has a variety of retailers. Some retailers do not allow posting of codes by users; in this case, check the comments to see if there is anything useful. Also check the maximum number of codes you can use per order, sometimes it is more than one!

Want to get paid to shop? It's possible! Sign up at **Ebates** and go there first to be directed to the retailer's page. It tracks your spending and sends you a quarterly check in the mail. It also posts coupon codes. If you are concerned about someone knowing your every click on a web page, be sure to read the fine print.

Now that you have bought all this stuff online, how do you keep track of it? Give **Slice** access to your email and it will constantly scan it for receipts and tracking numbers. Right on your smartphone with its free app you can receive an update about when a package is out for delivery and another when it has been delivered! The automated system sometimes has a hard time understanding your order, and for this it allows you to manually add the info; but for the most part it works pretty well. (Be sure to consider what types of emails go into the account before granting any site access to scan your email.)

If you are shopping in a brick-and-mortar store and forgot to bring your coupon, check the app **Coupon Sherpa.** The app lists many retailers and then directs you to their online coupons. Don't forget that if you have a smartphone, you can also pull up your email; and the casher can scan the coupon right from your email.

Want to make sure you're getting the best deal? Try the app **Shop-Savvy.** Simply scan the barcode of an item using your smartphone, and you will get prices for that product for local and online retailers. Keep in mind that you may have to pay shipping for online purchases unless you reach a minimum; so sometimes the prices are very low, and they make up for it with shipping.

Bonus tip: Some retailers accept expired printed coupons, so be sure to ask before throwing them out. Also, check to see if they take competitors' coupons!

Leslie Herberger is a highly experienced online shopper and loves a great deal! To support this fun habit, she is an executive assistant by day. Leslie also enjoys crafting and keeping up with the latest technology.

Bonus Shopping Tool: Larky

I just have to add this tool to Leslie's. I met the guys from **Larky** at a trade show, and the concept is intriguing. It's an iOS app that alerts you when you're entitled to a discount because of your membership in groups. For example, we have AAA; and if a local bakery gives a 10 percent discount on cupcakes to AAA members, my phone will ding when I drive by. So far I haven't used a discount, but it's cool that I have a central place to find them.

Shopping Tools at a Glance
(recommended tools in **bold**)

Coupon Sherpa	Coupon site and app for online and in-store purchases	Free	couponsherpa.com
Ebates	Coupon and online shopping site with cash-back offers	Free	ebates.com
Key Ring	**Android and iOS app that stores loyalty cards for easy access**	**Free**	**keyringapp.com**
Larky	Service that reveals discounts and deals you receive from your memberships	Free	larky.com
RetailMeNot	**Online coupon site**	**Free**	**retailmenot.com**
ShopSavvy	App that scans UPC codes to find reviews and deals	Free	shopsavvy.com
Slice	Service that monitors your email to track your shipped purchases	Free	slice.com

NerdHerd Favorite: Key Ring

Tired of digging through your wallet for your loyalty card at the grocery store to get $2 off your cupcakes? The **Key Ring** app (recommended by Chris B.) stores all your loyalty cards so the store can scan the info from your phone. Chris says, "Instead of inflating your wallet to 6 inches wide, you can save all your store points cards in this app on your phone."

Chapter 11

Relationship
Management

In this chapter:

Relationship management these days is much more than simply collecting leads. You need to keep track of relevant facts and statistics, play by the rules (both cultural and legal), and, most importantly, nurture the relationships by earning trust and loyalty.

Nurturing relationships and earning trust is what social networking is all about; but you can find plenty of books filled with recommendations for those tools, so I'll leave them out of here. But keep in mind that the tools in this chapter should go hand in hand with the plan you have to reach out to your community using social media.

Business Card Managers

bump

cardmunch

Contxts

Icon

ScanBizCards

My husband and I often lose our battle to keep the dining room table clean because of the dozens and dozens of business cards that pile up. We know we need to put them somewhere; but they have no real home, and they end up cluttering up our living areas. Over the years, I've had to keep my eye on the newest technology that will help us keep these piles at bay.

You can find dozens of smartphone apps that scan cards, but I cannot stand having to wait for the processing, then edit each field when the scanner misreads the teeny tiny print. So I insist that my card scanners have transcription verification by a human other than me.

LinkedIn's **cardmunch** sends your card to a real person somewhere in the world and returns it to you in great shape. Then you're just one button away from making your new contact a LinkedIn connection and integrating their information into your phone's address book.

Because I get piles of cards at a time after my presentations, I need a system that allows me to download the contacts into a spreadsheet, so

I pay about 18 cents a card to have someone at **ScanBizCards** verify the information.

If (OK, *when*) I forget my business cards, I use the virtual card I set up through **Contxts**. It's free and makes me look cool, or at least that's what I believe. I also agree with the recommendation of **Icon** from fellow speaker Thom Singer, the Networking Catalyst. Icon is a cloud-based digital business card that updates automatically with your social media integrations. The resulting personalized card site is attractive and always up to date.

The coolest contact exchange technology I've seen in a while is the **bump** app. When two people have the app, they simply bump their phones together to exchange information. And you can even bump yourself at your computer! Sorry, it's not nearly as fun as it sounds, but it is cool. You can visit bu.mp, choose a picture from your phone and bump the spacebar to transfer.

Business Card Tools at a Glance

(recommended tools in **bold**)

bump	iOS and Android app that trades virtual business cards by touching phones	Free	bu.mp/company
cardmunch	Card-scanning iOS app with human verification	Free	cardmunch.com
Contxts	**SMS business cards**	**Free**	**contxts.com**
Icon	Cloud-based digital business cards with social media integrations	Free for basic, or $4.99/month for Pro	icon.me
ScanBizCards	**Business card scanner for Android, Windows and iOS devices with optional human transcription**	**Free and paid apps available, and human transcription available for 18¢/card**	scanbizcards.com

NerdHerd Favorites: LinkedIn and cardmunch

Speaker and Sales Expert Alice Heiman (SmartSalesTips.com) calls LinkedIn and cardmunch essential for prospecting. Alice says, "Sign up for a free LinkedIn account and build your profile, then find everyone you know and connect. Then use the advanced search feature to build prospect lists."

Customer Relationship Management (CRMs)

Cirrus Insight

EQMS Lite

Salesforce

SugarCRM

timetonote

Zoho CRM

A customer relationship management system, commonly called a CRM, is really an electronic version of your company's address book. It's a database that keeps information about your connections, from names to birthdays to buying habits.

CRMs come in all shapes and sizes, both as stand-alone software and online. They can include just the basics—almost like a fancy format for your Excel spreadsheet. Today's CRMs now commonly include all kinds of helpful extras, such as social media integration, email management and marketing campaigns, sales tracking and project management.

I recently switched back to **Salesforce,** which is what we used when I worked for a vendor that sold conference recordings. I adored the system. It allowed us to track every email we sent, every proposal we created, every job we confirmed.

Chapter 11 ~ Relationship Management

At certain price levels, you can do everything from manage your contacts, track your communications and create email campaigns, to monitor sales (both the process and the signed contracts) and set up project management tools. In addition, it has hundreds of integrations in its AppExchange, many of which are in this book. I'm at the rock-bottom level: $5/month per user to track contacts, emails, events and calls. If my needs were more sales-oriented, the next level (where most of the goodies come in) is $25/month per user. Are you a nonprofit? Salesforce offers free licenses through their foundation.

My favorite integration for Salesforce helps my email management immensely. You can use an email address that Salesforce generates to bcc all your emails to your Salesforce account, but they show up in a big, uncategorized pile, so you end up doing twice the work. So I pay $9/month per user for my assistant and me to have the capability to connect all emails and attachments directly to the Salesforce contacts with the **Cirrus Insight** app.

A search on Google will give you hundreds of CRMs besides Salesforce, but **SugarCRM** often tops the lists. It's $35/month per user though; and that can add up quickly for a small staff, plus I'm wary of all the line items that say "optional upgrade." SugarCRM does list a self-hosted version that sounds like too much trouble. **EQMS Lite** is another download that gets high marks. **Zoho CRM** has a free version for offices of three or fewer, and its most expensive version is just $12/month per user. Another CRM, **timetonote,** is known as both a project management system and a CRM with attractive price points for small businesses. If I were looking for another system, this is probably where I'd start.

CRM Tools at a Glance

(recommended tools in **bold**)

Cirrus Insight	**App and browser add-ons that connect Salesforce to Gmail, Google Apps and Google Calendar**	**$9/month/user**	**cirrusinsight.com**
EQMS Lite	Downloadable CRM software for single user	Free for Lite version, or licensed version starts at $2/month. Note: You cannot upgrade directly to licensed version	spinsolite.com/ eqms_lite
Salesforce	**Hearty, flexible CRM for small-to-medium businesses and associations**	**Contact management for $5/user/month, or more traditional CRM levels starts at $25/user/month**	**salesforce.com**
SugarCRM	Well-established CRM with free, self-hosted community version	Free for self-hosted version, or starting at $35/month/user	sugarcrm.com
timetonote	**Web-based CRM and project management for groups**	**Free for basic level with 2 users, or premium version starts at $20/month**	**timetonote.com**
Zoho CRM	Online CRM with integrated social tools and optional mobile add-on	Free for up to 3 users, or lots more features for $12/user/month. Mobile add-on for $3/user/month	zoho.com/crm

Behind the Glasses: Choosing the Right CRM

In 2006, I broke off a long-term relationship and filled my heartbroken, empty hours on Friday and Saturday nights customizing my company's Salesforce system in every possible way (while angry single chick music played in the background). Templates, workflows, integrated apps, personalized screens—we're talking hours and hours of tear-stained work. Pathetic, yes, but oh so helpful for our company's efficiency.

When I left the company, I erroneously thought that I would need a CRM for my one-person copywriting business, and I shelled out hundreds of very precious start-up money for a CRM that worked through Microsoft Outlook. I never used it. Instead, I've come to realize that I use my email service system as a CRM—that's where all my contacts are listed, and I can see who is engaged with my information and contact them if needed.

The lesson I learned was that each business model and company has different needs, and not all CRMs fit every group. If you're not sure if you need a full-fledged CRM for your business, start out with a trial version, and make sure you try things that allow you to import and export your data.

Mass Email Services

Constant Contact

Emma

GetResponse

MailChimp

TinyLetter

VerticalResponse

I can't even remember how many years ago I started using email for newsletters and marketing. It was definitely way before it was cool, I think. And every year, I've seen the same types of statistics: The number of marketing emails is getting higher while the open and click rates are slowly sinking.

Don't get discouraged about your email marketing; help is on the way. You can choose from any number of free or bargain email and communication tools to help you stand out from the other zillion emails in the recipients' mailboxes to get your message out.

Way back when I was searching for a low-cost email service, I have to admit the **MailChimp** monkey turned me off. Sure, it's cute. But I didn't want cute. I wanted something professional. So I passed MailChimp by to choose **Constant Contact**.

Constant Contact is a great choice for do-it-yourself newsletters. It have a wide variety of templates, and its tracking is robust and reliable. What's more, I love its tips and newsletters, all designed to help you do a better job of standing out in people's email boxes.

But one of the most important things you can do to improve your newsletter is to test different sending times and subject lines. MailChimp makes it easy, with built-in A/B testing, while Constant Contact makes you create your own groups then download and upload and blah, blah, blah. Too much work. So I switched.

As it says on its website, MailChimp has "more email marketing tools than you can shake a banana at." Yeah, it's corny. But I'm willing to deal with corny for more capabilities. In addition, MailChimp integrates into some of my other tools, such as Sparkbooth (Page 229), my website and Facebook. It could also integrate with Salesforce if I wanted to capture all my newsletter subscribers as leads.

These days, you have lots of do-it-yourself email services besides MailChimp and Constant Contact. **GetResponse** is very reasonably priced and includes landing page help. **VerticalResponse** integrates postal mail campaigns and also has strong integrations with your social media accounts. I also like **Emma,** but only because of the cute, nerdy-girl logo. Emma also has a strong reputation, though it's pricier than most of its competitors.

If you are looking for more of a group email than a business newsletter, you could try MailChimp's free **TinyLetter,** a very basic email blast system for up to 2,000 subscribers.

Mass Email Services at a Glance (recommended tools in **bold**)

Constant Contact	Do-it-yourself newsletter service with integrated surveys and event management	$15 a month for up to 500 subscribers, then $30 a month for up to 2,500	constantcontact.com
Emma	Do-it-yourself email marketing with adorable logo	$30/month for up to 1,000 contacts	myemma.com
GetResponse	Do-it-yourself email marketing with optional landing page creator	$15/month for up to 1,000 contacts, and landing page creator options for $15/month	getresponse.com
MailChimp	**Robust and quirky do-it-yourself email newsletter service**	**Free for up to 2,000 subscribers and 12,000 emails a month**	**mailchimp.com**

Mass Email Services at a Glance (continued)

TinyLetter	Simple, free basic newsletters for small groups (less than 2000 subscribers)	Free	tinyletter.com
VerticalResponse	Do-it-yourself email newsletter service with social networking management and postcard services	Newsletters start at $10/month, and other services vary	verticalresponse.com

Nerdy Tip: Top Five Features to Look for in a Newsletter Service

1. **High integrity and a great reputation**

   The CAN-SPAM Act of 2003 established guidelines for promotional emails, and any legitimate email blast service will help you comply with the rules. Expect them to be very curious about your email lists because they want to keep spammers from subscribing to their service. The stricter they are, the better your chances of your mail getting through spam filters and into the inbox.

2. **Easy-to-use templates**

   I've seen a trend toward drag-and-drop newsletter building, which is really cool. This gives you lots of flexibility in building your own newsletter components. In addition to the empty templates, your service should offer pre-formatted options that will save you time and frustration.

3. **A/B testing capabilities**

   When it comes to maximizing your open/click rates, if you ain't testing, you ain't learning. Every time you send out a newsletter, you get a host of feedback about what people like and what they skip. A/B testing lets you figure out the best times, dates and subject lines to help you figure out what your recipients want to read.

4. **Help when you need it**

   Your provider should be an industry leader—an organization that provides benchmarking statistics as well as tips. MailChimp has a subject line analyzer as well as a spam scan and preview inspector for every possible email client. Constant Contact hosts free face-to-face seminars across the country and has a library of awesome tips.

5. **Integrated add-ons**

   Many of today's email providers let you embed surveys, invitations and social media buttons into your newsletters, saving you the trouble of building systems in one program then hopping back and forth to the newsletter draft to integrate them.

Email Alternatives

Paperless Post

Postagram

Punchbowl

My husband proposed to me in August of 2010; and after a negative experience with my practice husband, I wasn't about to let this good one get away. So we set the date a mere three months into the future. This gave me no time at all to get traditional invitations in the mail, so I chose the elegant email service **Paperless Post** to create what I thought were handsome replicas of a paper invitation

Come Celebrate with Us!

D.J. RAUSA
AND
BETH ZIESENIS
INVITE YOU TO THEIR
WEDDING CELEBRATION AND RING EXCHANGE

Paperless Post and **Punchbowl** send emails that look like envelopes and open dramatically when you click. You can send invitations, thank-you notes, birthday cards and all kinds of greetings through these services. You will probably see an uptick in both your open rates and ROI because they're different, fun and interactive.

Postagram is not an email at all. It's an extra-thick postcard with a cool punch-out picture. For about $1, you can simply upload a picture (or choose one from Instagram or Facebook), add an address then press a button. Within the week, your postcard will reach its destination; and again, you'll reap the benefit of standing out in an inbox.

Email Alternatives at a Glance

(recommended tools in **bold**)

Paperless Post	**Animated online cards and invitations integrated with Eventbrite**	**Free and paid cards, prices vary. Free cards available with free iOS app**	**paperlesspost.com**
Postagram	Instagram-connected service that sends attention-getting postcards	Starting at $1/ postcard for U.S. addresses	postagramapp.com
Punchbowl	Animated greeting cards with integrated event planning	Free cards and services, or ad-free levels start at $19/year	punchbowl.com

Guest Nerd: Networking Tools from Beth Bridges

Google Alerts

Nimble

popurls

Promtivate

Quora

These are not the networking tools to make computers play nice. This is about business and personal networking—face-to-face and via social media. The stronger and bigger the web of relationships you have, the more successful you will be at everything you do. Sociology nerds know about Dunbar's Number, which says our brains can only keep track of about 150 relationships at a time. But in your career and your lifetime, you'll meet and want to get to know hundreds of people. Far more than our unassisted brains can handle.

So I use technology to help me find the people I want to get to know, to learn more about them, to keep track of how to reach them and search out information to share that they will find valuable. From reminders to get back in touch to keeping the contact information handy to learning what they're up to, these sites help me build and keep a powerful network going.

Networking Tools at a Glance

Google Alerts	Create alerts for people you're interested in to learn when they are in the news and their accomplishments	Free	alerts.google.com
Nimble	Social CRM tool to manage contacts, communications, activities and even sales in one place	Free personal plan; business plan $15/month	nimble.com

Networking Tools at a Glance

popurls	Massive, customizable one-page news, vlog, link and social media aggregator	Free	popurls.com
Promptivate	Suggests whom to connect with and how, and reminds you to contact them	Free lite version; professional plan $14.95/month	promptivate.com
Quora	Share your knowledge by answering questions in your area of expertise	Free	quora.com

Beth Bridges is the Networking Motivator and author of the forthcoming book Networking on Purpose: A Simple Strategy for Building a Powerful and Profitable Business Network. *She has attended more than 2,300 networking events in the past 10 years and maintains relationships with hundreds of people in person and through social media. She shares networking tips and strategies at TheNetworkingMotivator.com.*

Chapter 12

Graphic Sources and Templates

have the utmost respect for graphic designers. They have the daunting task of converting your vision of a look into a beautiful, camera-ready graphic that you can use where you need it.

Graphic designers deserve to be well-paid employees and freelancers, but the challenge that many of us face is that we don't have the budget to have them with us for our every little want and need—or they're so good and so busy that they don't have the time.

That's why I love, love, love these graphic sources, which can give us many tools to create our own graphics and materials, without the help of a graphic designer.

Royalty-Free Stock Images

Way back in the day, when small-business folks like me needed a nice image for our blogs, marketing or other stuff, were forced to either, umm, *borrow*, an image we found on the web (which was often low-resolution, thus bad for printing) or pony up hundreds for royalty-free stock photography from high-end sites such as Getty Images.

But nowadays, there's no end to the number of so-called microstock sites—online marketplaces where freelance photographers and multimedia artists, both amateur and professional, sell their images for a fraction of the cost at the high-end sites.

Characteristics of Stock Image Sites

Almost every site has the following:

- ✔ Ka-bunches of searchable images, including photos, illustrations, vector graphics, audio clips and videos

✔ Advanced search engines that let you fine-tune your searches, such as

- A horizontal picture of a man at a computer with a white background and copy space on the left
- An illustration of a house with no people in the graphic and red as a primary color

✔ Subscription or credit-based pricing tiers (Some also have prices listed.)

✔ Multiple sizes and resolutions

✔ Clear guidelines on image use

✔ Collection tools such as lightboxes that allow you to select several options into a library to share with others for the final decision.

The increase in competition is both good and bad. It's good because you have such an amazing database of images to choose from, and the competition means the prices stay reasonable. But having so many sites means that you can spend hours and hours (my Friday nights) searching multiple sites and comparing prices and looks. Believe me, this can drive you insane and suck up your time.

What You Can Do With a Royalty-Free Image

Most of the sites will include the following uses with a standard purchase. Check the fine print for individual restrictions, such as the number of impressions that the license includes. For example, if I sell more than half a million of these books, I have to pay for an extended license of the awesome jumping nerd guy on the front cover.

✔ Website

✔ Emails

✔ Business cards

✔ Printed and electronic marketing and business materials

✔ Letterhead

✔ Book and e-book covers

✔ Product packaging

✔ Posters

What You Can't Do With a Royalty-Free Image

Again, each site may differ, but here are some common license restrictions.

- ✔ Don't use in your logos or trademarks
- ✔ Don't make it look like the model in the image is endorsing your product or has mental or physical health issues, drug problems, etc.
- ✔ Don't share or give away your purchased images

Buying Extended Rights to Images

If you do want to get a bunch of coffee mugs made, you can purchase extended rights for a few hundred bucks. Again, check the license agreements for the specific requirements of your images.

Stock Image and Music Sites

123RF

AudioJungle

ClipartOf

Dreamstime

Flickr Creative Commons

iStockphoto

Morguefile

SXC

VectorStock

Wikimedia Commons

The prices on these sites vary greatly. **iStockphoto** used to be my first choice; but in the past year, it seems to be inching toward the uncomfortable end of my budget. So these days, I comparison shop, looking for both variety and better pricing.

This cupcake picture appears on many microstock sites, and the prices for the same high-res version vary wildly. In all cases, I used the calculation of the minimum number of credits I needed—if you buy more credits, the prices can go down. On iStockphoto, you'll pay $21 for this cupcake. It's $3 less on **Dreamstime,** but you'll pay just $5 on **123RF.** (Guess where I shop most often!)

All three of those sites include multimedia clips as well as vector graphics, but I have some specialty sites for other formats. For royalty-free music, I head to **AudioJungle** (another site from Envato, which owns my favorite design template site, GraphicRiver). And I like **ClipartOf** for clipart and illustrations and **Vector-Stock** for, believe it or not, vectors.

In addition to the paid sites, you can find stock images for free. I don't have the patience or the free time to track down quality freebies, but some of my readers have had great luck with these resources:

- ✔ Free bin on the paid sites

- ✔ Flickr Creative Commons (multiple use scenarios—check the fine print)

- ✔ SXC (short for stock.xchng, owned by Getty Images)

- ✔ Morguefile

- ✔ Wikimedia Commons (where I found this cupcake image)

Stock Image Search Tools

Compfight

Everystockphoto

Google Image Search

Need help finding a bargain? If you type "single cupcake white background stock photo" into the **Google Images** search engine, you will find stock shots from a bunch of sites at once, rather than having to go to each.

You can also select a photo in a Google search and drag it to the top of the page to search by image attributes. (See a how-to video here: nerdy.bz/GoogleImageSearch.)

Compfight is a great way to search through Creative Commons and will even help you provide the proper attribution on your site or other material. **Everystockphoto** is also a great resource for free images.

Behind the Glasses: Finding Graphic Design Help

Can't find the perfect image? Make your own! Freelance sites Elance and Fiverr have artists and experts who can turn your vision into reality at a reasonable rate (See Outside Help, Page 243).

Royalty-Free Sources at a Glance (recommended tools in **bold**)

123RF	**Low-priced royalty-free image site**	**Varies**	**123rf.com**
AudioJungle	**Royalty-free music site from respected provider Envato**	**Ranges from sound effects for $1 to music collections for $30 and more**	**audiojungle.net**
ClipartOf	**Royalty-free illustration and clipart site**	**Varies**	**clipartof.com**
Compfight	Image search engine for Flickr Creative Commons	Free	compfight.com
Dreamstime	Moderately priced royalty-free image site	Varies	dreamstime.com
Everystockphoto	Search engine for free stock images	Free	everystockphoto.com
Flickr Creative Commons	Flickr collection of images that may be used with attribution for personal and commercial use	Free	flickr.com/ creativecommons
Google Image Search	**Robust image search engine**	**Free**	**images.google.com**
iStockphoto	Well-established royalty-free image site	Varies	istockphoto.com
Morguefile	Free royalty-free stock images	Free	morguefile.com
SXC	Getty Images-owned free royalty-free images site	Free	sxc.hu
VectorStock	Royalty-free image site for vector graphics	Varies	vectorstock.com
Wikimedia Commons	Free royalty-free image site in a Wikipedia style	Free	commons.wikimedia.org

Font Identification Tools

Identifont

WhatTheFont!

Wordmark.it

Eureka! You've discovered the perfect font for your next marketing piece on a political postcard that arrived in the mail. But what's the font name, and where can you find it?

Two of my favorite free tools can help, and they both have names I love. **Identifont** has a step-by-step wizard that takes you through a series of questions about the font, such as where the squiggle goes on the capital "Q." It'll even help if you have only a few letters to work with (like a flier headline). Another great search engine is its picture search tool, which combs picture- and symbol-based fonts to help you find that perfect dingbat of a pair of nerdy glasses.

Grab a graphic of a mystery font you'd love to identify, and upload it to **WhatTheFont!** The site will analyze the graphic and make recommendations to identify your font. If you don't find a match, try visiting the WhatTheFont Forum, where it says, "Cloak-draped font enthusiasts around the world will help you out!"

One more tip to help you find the perfect font. Have you ever spent a half-hour in Microsoft Word scrolling through your installed fonts one by one to find the perfect look for a document? **Wordmark.it** is a clever web tool lets you write a few words for a preview then loads your fonts into the site so you can see them all at once. The site lets you choose your favorites then filter them to see your top choices together. It's 100 percent free and super easy to use.

Font Sources

dafont

Font Squirrel

Fontifier

FontSpace

Google Web Fonts

Kevin and Amanda

YourFonts

dafont.com is my very favorite place on the web to find fonts with a little pizazz to add a little something extra to a look and feel. I love putting my word or phrase into the custom preview box and the searching by theme (cartoon, curly, calligraphy, handwritten) to find just the right look. Most are free for personal use, and many are just plain free. An awesome resource for any do-it-yourself graphic designer.

Font Squirrel is another great resource, though it's my second choice because it doesn't let you preview your text. The cool thing about the resources on this site is that they're all free for commercial use, so you won't have the letdown of finding the perfect font on dafont and then having to give it up because it's just for personal use. **FontSpace** is another great font repository, and **Kevin and Amanda** specializes in handwriting tools.

The site doesn't have a preview button, so you have to scroll through the fonts; but the collection of fun handwritten fonts is impressive.

And if you're looking to add a little snazzy-ness to your website, you can find new fonts that will work on the web at **Google Web Fonts.**

You don't have to browse thousands of fonts to find the perfect look. You can make your own. Tired of writing piles of thank-you notes by hand? Create a computer font with your own handwriting with **Fontifier** or **YourFonts**. Both sites let you download the templates, fill in the letters then scan in the results. Free to preview, then purchase and install. You can also create fonts with common phrases, such as "Best wishes," or "Thanks for the cupcake!"

Keep in mind that this technique works better on printed or block characters than cursive. It may take you a couple of tries to fill in the template correctly. You may not fool your grandmother into thinking that you handwrote your Christmas update, but your own font can be a great touch for letters, thank-you notes, scrapbooks and journals.

Font Tools at a Glance

(recommended tools in **bold**)

dafont	Archive of freely downloadable fonts with awesome preview tool	Free	dafont.com
Font Squirrel	**Free fonts for commercial use (no instant previews)**	**Free**	**fontsquirrel.com**
Fontifier	Handwriting font tool with options to create signatures and other phrases	$9	fontifier.com
FontSpace	Free font collection with previews	Free	fontspace.com
Google Web Fonts	Directory of fonts you can install on websites	Free	google.com/webfonts
Identifont	**Online wizard to identify typefaces**	**Free**	**identifont.com**
Kevin and Amanda	Directory of fun handwriting fonts	Free	kevinandamanda.com/fonts
WhatTheFont!	**Online tool and iOS app to identify fonts**	**Free**	**myfonts.com/WhatTheFont**
Wordmark.it	**Online previews of the fonts on your computer**	**Free**	**wordmark.it**
YourFonts	Custom font with your handwriting	$9.95 for basic, or $14.95 for two pages of characters	yourfonts.com

Chapter 13

Graphics Creators

In this chapter:

Infographics and Timelines

An infographic is a visual presentation of facts, ideas or statistics, usually characterized by fun graphics, colorful themes and few words. In today's graphic-happy world, infographics are incredibly popular and can often go viral on social media sites. You're more likely to have people share an infographic with the highlights of your latest survey than a 16-page white paper with all the details.

Infographics are all the rage for communicating facts and trends instantly, but they can cost a fortune. Back when I was a copywriter, I worked with several companies that commissioned infographics from design companies, at $1,500 a pop or more. Thank goodness for the many websites that have popped up that allow us to use flexible templates to make our own.

Infographics

Easelly

Infogram

Piktochart

Venngage

Visual.ly

Visual.ly is one of a couple of innovative companies that are offering instant infographics using fun templates. With this site, you just link the template to your Facebook or Twitter account, and in seconds you have an amusing analysis.

Here's a section from my Twitter analysis. Geeky grin indeed!

My first infographic (available on the AskBethZ Pinterest board) was an analysis of the elements of the perfect nerdy office, which I put together with **Piktochart.** I have to tell you that it takes patience—a lot of patience. With its templates, things jump around, move mysteriously, and are challenging to align and move. But the overall result was quite pleasing. Piktochart has been around for quite a while, and early in 2013 it upped its value by making its infographics searchable so that you can help your search engine optimization (SEO) efforts.

Venngage is an interesting tool for internal reports and data analyses, but I haven't played with it. **Easelly** was still in beta in 2013, and I found the interface pretty easy to work with. **Infogram** only has four templates for infographics, but its charts and graphs are quite attractive.

Timelines

Preceden

TimeRime

Timetoast

Timelines are great ways to present time-dependent data, such as the history of an association or milestones in the life of a retiring chairman of the board. Students can also use them in reports and research. Online timelines have a huge advantage over the 8½-x-11-inch sheets we taped together and rolled up to turn in for school projects. You can add videos, interactive buttons, cool scrolling and pop-ups to a multimedia snapshot of time.

Timetoast is the best free choice, but **Preceden** and **TimeRime** have great pricing for students and educators.

Infographics and Timelines at a Glance (recommended tools in **bold**)

Easelly	New startup infographic site	Free in beta	easel.ly
Infogram	**Interactive charts and infographics for free**	**Free**	**infogr.am**
Piktochart	**Custom infographics at a bargain price (or free)**	**Free for basic, or subscriptions start at $29/month.**	**piktochart.com**
Preceden	Quick timelines for presentations with special access for teachers	Add five events to timeline for free, or one-time payment of $29 for unlimited	preceden.com
TimeRime	Online timeline creator with collaboration	Free for regular features, or Pro lets you custom brand and embed on your own sites	timerime.com
Timetoast	Free timelines for presentations and reports	Free	timetoast.com
Venngage	Infographics for internal reports and analyses	Free in beta	venngage.com
Visual.ly	**Instant social media infographics for free**	**Free for templates**	**visual.ly**

Image Generators

Woohoo! You've reached my favorite category of tools. OK, I have lots of favorite categories, but this is definitely in the top 10.

Image generator sites and apps are silly, strange, interesting, useful, instant, helpful and fun. The concept is simple: choose a picture template or frame, add your own photo or logo, and press a button. Your image will be placed into the frame, and POOF—you have an instant graphic to use in newsletters, online, in marketing material—wherever you need it.

Here are a handful of ways you can use these generators:

Create seasonal accents for newsletters around holidays...

Brand your video or learning series...

Or just make someone laugh…

Here's a partial list of some of my favorite image generator sites, but the best way to see the full range is to visit my Pinterest Board (pinterest.com/askbethz).

funnywow.com	**keepcalm-o-matic.co.uk**	photo505.com
funphotobox.com	loonapix.com	**photofacefun.com**
glassgiant.com	lunapic.com	photofunia.com
imagechef.com	pho.to	signgenerator.org

Word Art Tools

Tagxedo textagon	**Tagxedo** is the ultimate over-the-top crowd pleaser! It's my very favorite place to play with words. Tagxedo can either scan text or sites for words, or you can create a list of your own.

The awesomeness of Tagxedo is only limited by your imagination. You can change the shape of your art, use your own fonts, customize the colors and spend all day long playing around with it to create a beautiful graphic.

Although you can't save your work, Tagxedo lets you download your graphics in a number of formats, including print-friendly resolutions. If you are creating Tagxedo art for commercial use (to offer for sale, for example), contact the site owner for licensing pricing. I also enjoy **textagon** for playing with words—so easy you can make art in the bathtub (Page 178).

Word Art Tools at a Glance

(recommended tools in **bold**)

Tagxedo	Word cloud generator site	Free	tagxedo.com
textagon	Site and iOS app that turns words into art	Free	textagon.com

NerdHerd Thumbs Up: Tagxedo

Jennifer V. Wetherbee, a Rodan + Fields independent consultant, loves Tagxedo for its ability to organize words from websites into cool designs and colors. "It is so easy to use, and any picture can be downloaded to use at the object for your words to mold around."

Guest Nerd: More Word Cloud Generators from Dr. Michelle Post

Tagul

WordItOut

Wordle

WordSift

A word cloud is a visual representation of keywords from a specific concept, theory, industry, speech, lecture, letters, love notes and/or description of an individual's skills/abilities. A word cloud consists of a combination of keywords that can be made into different shapes and sizes. All of the word cloud generators described here are FREE and are online, there is need to download any type of application to your computer.

Wordle is a simple tool to use that generates great graphical word clouds. In the words of the creator of Wordle is, ". . . a toy for generating 'word clouds' from text that you provide." Wordle.net allows you to copy and paste a block of text into an online window and with the simple click of a button a word cloud is generated from the text in the window. Words that appear more than once in the block of text will be larger than single frequency words.

Wordle.net allows the user to either randomly generate the word cloud or customize the word cloud with different layouts, fonts, and colors. You can then save the new word cloud to the public gallery or print it. No sign up is necessary.

Tagul has the same functions as Wordle plus more: text within text, rollover effects and custom shapes just to name a few. Tagul does require the end user to sign-up with its site, but it is still free to use.

Additional word cloud generators are WordItOut and WordSift, but these are not all that are available. There are word cloud generators just for children and others just for analyzing text.

Word Cloud Generators at a Glance

Wordle	Online word cloud generator with public gallery, fonts, layouts and colors	Free	wordle.net
Tagul	Online word cloud generator (registration required) with fonts, colors, shapes and rollovers	Free	tagul.com
WordItOut	Online word cloud generator with the claim that it has more settings than any other generator	Free	worditout.com
WordSift	Online word cloud generator focused on analyzing text to find the important words from a block of text such as a speech or lecture	Free	wordsift.com

Michelle Post, Ph.D., MBA

Dr. Michelle Post teaches and speaks in both corporate and academia on a variety of subjects that include social media, generations in the workplace/classroom, leadership, organizational development, human resource development, technology in education and personal development. She is the author of three books: Heaven Has Tea Parties, Building Your Adjunct Platform *and* Reflections of Weekly Words, *all available on Amazon.com.*

Animated Generators

Animoto

GoAnimate

PowToon

ToonDoo

XtraNormal

Once you read this page, you should tear it off and eat it so none of your co-workers or competitors ever learn the secret behind your seemingly effortless awesomeness.

Animoto is one of those tools that makes the crowds go "WOW" and look at you in wonder.

The premise is incredibly simple: Gather 10 or more pictures, throw in a title and choose a theme and soundtrack—then push a button. PRESTO! Animoto instantly creates a perfectly timed, perfectly professional, perfectly awesome video that can showcase your event, your boss's retirement, your kid's prom preparations, your company's products—you name it. And when you share the video, your audience will whisper, "Wow, how did she do that?"

Animoto is just plain cool, with an intuitive interface and fun graphics. It's won all kinds of awards including a Crunchy and a Webby, and you can even use it to create high-quality DVD videos.

The mobile apps (Android and iOS) make the tool even more awesome. Snap pictures of your exhibitors for a dynamic thank-you video at the closing session, or make a montage on the fly of the award winners from your luncheon. Everything you need to produce the video is on your mobile device, and it takes just minutes to render.

The music and themes are built into the program, or you can use your own soundtrack (if you own the rights). It has quite a few templates to choose from, and every once in a while it throws in another.

You know those awesome stop-motion videos that startup companies with marketing budgets create to showcase their products? Design companies charge THOUSANDS to create these custom videos, but now they have a strong competitor!

I am now officially in love with **PowToon.** When I say in love, I mean head over heels. The service lets you use easy-to-manipulate figures to create your own stop-motion videos. It takes a little finagling to get used to the interface; but once you understand the basics, it's pretty easy to create a video, like this one on how to pronounce "Ziesenis."

✔ Nerdy.bz/lastname

Another way to liven up your online presence is to create an animated cartoon. The two best tools for this are **GoAnimate** and **XtraNormal**. I've played around with both tools several times, and they're really cool. You pick everything from the background to the characters to the expressions on their faces and the way they point at each other. You type the dialog and pick the funny robotic voice of your actors—or even record your own voices for a more personalized video. A short piece without a lot of fancy touches might take you less than half an hour to create, or you could probably spend hours on the little details.

Both GoAnimate and XtraNormal have free-ish plans, which means you can play around with some very basic templates before shelling out any money. If you're going to use the videos for your business, you'll need to consider the subscription levels for professional use, which start at about $25/month.

If you want to add a little twist to your marketing, make a fun cartoon. **Toon-Doo** has templates and characters that you can drag and drop into a variety of cartoon formats. You can even put several cartoons together into a flippable cartoon book that reminds me of Issuu (Page 200). My ToonDoo, Nerd Life, actually became a site favorite for a couple of months.

NerdHerd Thumbs Up: animoto and PowToon

NerdHerders love to make engaging videos. Johanne Stogran from the Botanical Society of America creates videos with animoto. "It's fun and easy to use and makes me look good!," she says. And PowToon is a favorite of both Denise Whitehead from Glades Electric Cooperative and Matthew Nicholas from the Illinois Physical Therapy Association. Denise used PowToon to create an important message about legislative changes to their members—to the amazement of her colleagues.

Animated Generators at a Glance (recommended tools in **bold**)

Animoto	**Instant multimedia masterpieces from pictures, videos and text**	**Free for videos up to 30 seconds, or starting at $30/year for longer videos and more templates**	**animoto.com**
GoAnimate	Easy animation tool	Free for basic, then starting at $25/month for business use	goanimate.com
PowToon	**Super cool animated video and presentation tool**	**Free for branded videos, or pay per HD download. Subscriptions start at $20/month**	**powtoon.com**
ToonDoo	Cartoon and avatar maker	Free for online images, or small charge to download high-res graphics for printing	toondoo.com
XtraNormal	3D animated movie maker	$50/month for unlimited professional or à la carte	xtranormal.com

Templates

Codecanyon

Graphicriver

Microsoft Office Templates

Themeforest

Woothemes

Not long ago, I decided my presentations needed a facelift. I threw out the old Slide 1, Slide 2 format of my old PowerPoint and created a presentation that appeared to pull new screens into view with a thin line. Instead of just appearing, items flipped in, popped up and pushed the previous graphics out.

The very first time I unveiled the format, audience members started tracking me down after the session to demand my secret. "That can't be boring old PowerPoint, can it?" they asked. "Why yes, it is," I answered, "but I cheated!"

My secret? Pre-made templates, purchased for $10 to $40, that you can customize and adopt to transform your boring presentations. I spent less than $100 on a handful of presentation templates that I use for various presentation types to give my sessions a little extra flair.

And my website? Another template. And the cool plug-ins on my site? More little extras purchased from these sites. To me they're a small-business owner's secret ingredient for materials that go beyond the normal. Instead of paying for custom materials, you can simply find a professional-grade starting point and customize.

If you don't want to pay anything at all, it's easy to Google "free presentation template" or other terms to find collections. I also have found fairly nice starting places in the template communities supported by **Microsoft Office** (just start a new document from a template in MS Office software, and explore online templates to see the freebies). But a small investment in a professional template often gives me a high-quality framework that elevates my look without tons of customization. You can also find free and inexpensive third-party templates for other office suites, such as Google Docs and Apple's iWork programs.

The best collection of template tools that I've discovered comes from several sites in the Envato family. Envato is the company behind Freelance Switch, a website that helps freelancers run their businesses. All the Envato sites have the same login and payment system, so you can buy credits on one site and use them on others.

Envato's collections include **GraphicRiver,** which contains many categories of templates for small businesses, including print templates, infographics, logos and presentation templates. It also has **ThemeForest** for website templates and plug-ins, and **CodeCanyon** for widgets and other fancy add-ons. If you're just looking for WordPress (Page 47) themes, I have purchased several from **WooThemes.**

Templates at a Glance
(recommended tools in **bold**)

CodeCanyon	Professional website add-ons	Varies	codecanyon.net
GraphicRiver	**Professional templates for websites, presentations, print and logos**	**Varies**	**graphicriver.net**
Microsoft Office Templates	**Random selection of free templates for MS Office products**	**Free**	**office.microsoft.com/ templates**
ThemeForest	Professional website templates	Varies	themeforest.net
WooThemes	**Professional WordPress templates**	**Varies**	**woothemes.com**

Nerdy Tip:
All about Templates

Why Pay for a Template?

Templates can save you tons of time and money when you need a custom look. Even when you're working with a designer, you can purchase a starting point that captures the direction you hope to go and have the designer dial it in.

Avoiding Template Troubles

Many are inflexible and won't let you truly customize. If you keep finding roadblocks, sometimes it's best to just give in and stop trying to customize or find another resource.

Make sure you check the format before you purchase a template. If all you have is Microsoft Word, Adobe InDesign files won't work for you.

Spending just $10 or $20 instead of choosing a free template can mean a world of difference in the functionality and professionalism of the template.

Online and App Design Tools

Brother Creative Center

Checkthis

MyCreativeShop

Over

Phoster

Tweak

Vistaprint

Most of the templates in this chapter are files that you download and modify in your own software or on your site, but I'm also infatuated with drag-and-drop online and app tools that help you create posters and more without having the software.

For an instant poster, try the **Phoster** app (iOS), which lets you add your own pictures and text to its templates for printable and shareable posters for events and ads. As of this writing, its templates were pretty rigid, but they can be great for a quick sign. You can also use **Checkthis** (Page 48), a site and app that create "social posters" you can share online. I also like an app called **Over**, which lets you artfully arrange words over a picture for a modern poster look.

A hidden online template resource comes from printing sites, such as **Brother Creative Center, Tweak, MyCreativeShop** and the ubiquitous **Vistaprint**. All have a plethora of designs you can personalize online. Brother offers the service for free in hopes that you'll use a Brother printer to print it. Tweak is free, but the PDF download has very robust and obtrusive watermarks, so the only thing you can do with it is print it through Tweak.

Like Tweak, Vistaprint lets you design for free and download a watermarked PDF (which it charges you $1.99 for). I'd definitely go for Tweak over Vistaprint since the latter's designs are incredibly generic and definitely not a step up for your professional look. MyCreativeShop also wants you to print with it, but it charges $20 a month for its design software so you can download high-quality documents and use them how you wish. Both include access to a large library of stock photography, which helps you avoid the cost of buying images (see Page 152).

Online and App Design Tools at a Glance (recommended tools in **bold**)

Brother Creative Center	**Free online print design site from Brother printers**	**Free**	**brother.com/ creativecenter**
Checkthis	**Social poster maker (online and iOS app)**	**Free**	**checkthis.com**
MyCreativeShop	Subscription-based online design site with robust template and stock image library	$19.95/month	mycreativeshop.com
Over	iOS app that creates a poster-type look for your photos with creative text overlay	$1.99	madewithover.com
Phoster	**iOS app for creating printable and sharable posters**	**$1.99**	**phoster.bucketlabs.net**
Retromatic	**iPad app for vintage posters**	**$1.99**	**Available in the App Store**
Tweak	Online designer for printed matter	Free to design, but only option is to print your materials through Tweak	tweak.com
Vistaprint	Online print designer with basic customization and designs	Free to design, but no downloads for electronic use	vistaprint.com

Behind the Glasses: Bathtub Apps

I like spending time in the bathtub almost as much as I like eating cupcakes. If I could, I'd relocate my home office to the bathtub with a waterproof keyboard and a flat-screen monitor sealed into the tile. But since that seems frivolous, I make do by sealing my iPad into a double-zipper gallon freezer bag. Sometimes I watch live TV with my Time Warner Cable app, but other times I'm all about app research. The iPad graphic generators are great for bath time, and I have created several dozen images while soaking. My favorites are **Retromatic**, Phoster, Keep Calm poster makers (various), textagon and PhotoFunia.

Buttons

Art Text

Cool Text

Da Button Factory

VerticalResponse Button Builder

When you need a fast "Click Here" button for your electronic communications, nothing beats the ease of **Cool Text.** An oldie but a goodie, this ad-supported site lets you start with a pre-formatted button or styled text. Then you can customize the heck out of it, like I did with this "nerd out" button, changing the font, color, size and shape. Its font collection is huge, and the output is a nice resolution for online applications.

Need something for your website? **Vertical-Response Button Builder** lets you make online buttons in seconds. I also love **Da Button Factory,** mostly because of its name.

If you have a Mac, I have another awesome tool. For about a kabillion reasons, I switched from PC to Mac in 2012. One of the main benefits has been the access to thousands of free and bargain apps from the App Store. I stumbled upon **Art Text** (Mac and Windows 8) and fell in love. It has a lite version for free, but I upgraded almost immediately to the full version for about $20.

I absolutely adore playing with this tool. In just a few minutes I can create a 3D, super fancy "click here" button for my newsletter. I also designed this cool header and some other fun stuff.

Weekly Tech Tools and Tips

Buttons at a Glance
(recommended tools in **bold**)

Art Text 2	Button and special text generator app for Mac or Windows 8	Free for Lite version, or $19.99 for full	belightsoft.com/ products/arttext
Cool Text	Easy-to-use web button generator	Free	cooltext.com
Da Button Factory	Online button generator	Free	dabuttonfactory.com
VerticalResponse Button Builder	Simple online button builder	Free	buttons.verticalresponse.com

Chapter 14

. . . .

Image and Multimedia Editing

Isn't it frustrating when you have the perfect 2-x-3-inch picture of your product, but you have a 2-x-2-inch space on your website to add something? And isn't it even more frustrating when you don't have your own tools to fix it, so you have to wait until your graphics person has five minutes or your cousin from design school returns your email?

The problem with acquiring the tools you need is money. Or at least it used to be before you picked up this book. The most powerful tools come with the most powerful prices—hundreds of dollars per license for software that most of us will rarely need to use.

Back before I became free-tool enlightened, I would try to get by with Microsoft Window's free Paint tool to clean up and fix graphics pixel by pixel; and my graphics ended up fuzzy, uneven messes. But then I discovered some completely amazing and unbelievably free applications and websites that give me almost all the capabilities of the expensive tools without any of the cost. And if you do need the full version of the expensive tools, you have more options than ever to save money.

Downloadable Image Editors

GIMP

Gimpshop

Inkscape

Pixelmator

Vector Magic

GIMP might be the king when it comes to open-source Adobe Photoshop competitors. Its unfortunate name comes from its humble beginnings as a student project at Berkeley in the mid-1990s. Two guys worked together to create the General Image Manipulation Program, which attracted a loyal following and passionate coders who kept it going.

Today the GIMP community still works together to upgrade the program, release new versions and get the word out. Download GIMP to manipulate photos with its many plug-ins and extensions, and visit the forums for lively and informative conversations about tips and bug fixes. Well, lively conversations for nerds.

A note for experienced Photoshop users—the GIMP interface is a little different; and some Photoshoppers get a little frustrated. You might try **Gimpshop** for a more Photoshop-like experience, or go for **Pixelmator** for the Mac, which is what I use for my desktop editing.

For advanced printing projects, you may need a more robust tool. Most digital graphics files look great on the screen but don't print out well. That's why your designer will ask for vector files instead of JPEGs for a print job. **Vector Magic** is an inexpensive way to convert a bitmap graphic into a scalable vector graphic. It's free to upload your graphic and try it out, and you get two free conversions once you sign up. Use the online version or download the application to your desktop. You can also download the open-source vector editor **Inkscape**.

NerdHerd Favorite: Luminance HDR

My running buddy Eric Witmayer is a proud nerd who often shares great tools. He likes **Luminance HDR,** an advanced editor for photography that specializes in high-dynamic-range imaging, which has to do with enhancing the range between the lightest and darkest parts of the image.

NerdHerd Thumbs Up: GIMP

Michael Shaw from the Community Associations Institute calls GIMP a "free and fantastic image creation, manipulation and editing tool."

Online Image Editors

PicMonkey

Pixlr

Splashup

Sumopaint

Pixlr is my favorite online image editor, with a Flash-based uploader that allows you to edit from any computer without having the software. It's incredibly amazing, easy to use, fast, convenient and awesome. Does that make it clear how I feel?

I used to be afraid an Internet hiccup that would make me lose my work, but truthfully it's become one of my most valuable tools. Download the Pixlr Grabber extension for Firefox or Chrome, and you can right-click on any picture to instantly edit it in Pixlr. It is now integrated with Google Drive so you can save your images into the cloud immediately.

Pixlr Editor has many of the same features as Photoshop, and the Express version is perfect for easy, immediate editing. It also has a fun Instagram-type filter and morphing tool, Pixlr-o-matic, which you can get online and on smart devices.

The company celebrated its fourth anniversary in 2012, and 3D design software giant Autodesk purchased it not long ago. This worries me a little because I want this tool to stay free, easy and available. I'm thinking it'll start making money through its mobile apps, since it is making quite a name for itself in that arena these days, winning an award for the best Android picture editor and being called an Instagram competitor in some high-profile blogs.

Before Pixlr, my first online image editor love was Picnik. I never really got over it when Google bought it in 2010. But in 2012, two of the original engineers from Picnik started **PicMonkey,** another fun, free, fantastically easy online photo-editing site. As with Picnik, PicMonkey has many user-friendly tools to resize, revamp and re-engineer a graphic in minutes. It has a robust free version that is supported with ads; or you can upgrade for $5 a month for no ads and more effects, fonts and other goodies. **Sumopaint** and **Splashup** also have robust features and easy-to-use interfaces.

Image Editors at a Glance

(recommended tools in **bold**)

GIMP	Open-source Photoshop-like download	Free	gimp.org
Gimpshop	Open-source Photoshop-like download with a more Photoshop-type interface	Free	gimpshop.com
Inkscape	**Open-source, down-loadable vector editor**	**Free**	**inkscape.org**
Luminance HDR	High-dynamic-range imaging download for enhancing photography	Free	qtpfsgui.sourceforge.net
PicMonkey	Online photo editor from the makers of Picnik	Basic editing features and filters for free, or starting at $33/year for full version	picmonkey.com
Pixelmator	Downloadable image editor for Mac	$14.99	pixelmator.com
Pixlr	**Free online Photoshop competitor**	**Free**	**pixlr.com**
Splashup	Online graphic editors—both advanced and lite	Free	splashup.com

Image Editors at a Glance (continued)

Sumopaint	Online photo editor with 3D coolness	Free for basic, or up to $19 for a lifetime license with downloadable version	sumopaint.com
Vector Magic	Online vector conversion site	$7.95/month for online application, or one-time fee of $295 for download	vectormagic.com

Nerdy Tip: Open an Adobe Illustrator File

Ever get an Adobe Illustrator file from a designer and couldn't open it? You have the power! Just launch your regular old (free) Adobe Reader application, then search for the .ai file. You'll see the file just like you had the full program!

Multimedia Editors

Audacity

BUZZcard

Ezvid

iMovie

Windows Movie Maker

YouTube Video Editor

Warning: When you play around with the tools in this section, plan to spend a long, long time making teeny, tiny adjustments and biting your lip. Or maybe it's just me who gets lost in the infinite number of adjustments and enhancements that you can add to a multimedia file.

Free tools for multimedia editing these days go far beyond simple trimming or adding a title slide. If you have the patience (and develop the talent), you can create slick videos and audio clips that can look as if a professional did them.

I have to admit that although I've created several pretty good little movies and some acceptable audio clips, I have a reputation for being impatient (just ask my husband—and my parents—and my sister). So if a project looks like it will push me toward a cupcake binge with frustration, I will farm it out to an expert on Fiverr or Elance (see Outside Help chapter, Page 243).

If I had to choose the free tool that I respect the most, award-winning **Audacity** would win. It's a fully functional, incredibly professional, easy-to-use, and multilingual audio editor and recorder. It's been around for as long as I've been seeking free stuff, and it's updated for every conceivable platform on a regular basis.

Now, just because I love this tool doesn't mean I've mastered it. If you're not used to editing audio or messing with all kinds of levers and knobs to get the best sound, the interface may be confusing. But I have managed to use it to record some professional-sounding clips and do some basic editing for length and clarity.

When it comes to multimedia editing on my Mac, I have a love/hate relationship with **iMovie**. On one hand, I've been able to use the templates to create some completely awesome videos, both personal and professional. But on the other hand, every single time I use it, I wind up frowning and frustrated because of my own ineptness in video editing as well as the program's insatiable hunger for fine tuning.

When I am patient enough, the results can be impressive (see the samples), but I always end up taking about three times as long as I want to on a "quick" video for my business.

Windows Movie Maker may already be on your PC because it often comes with Windows Essentials, or you can download whatever version you need from the Microsoft site. The software puts powerful video-editing capabilities in everyone's hands, even if you're not particularly artsy.

Ezvid is another movie editor for Windows, with the added bonus of a screencapture tool (see more screencapture resources, Page 79).

I created several pretty nice pieces with relative ease. Yes, you're going to get a little frustrated with the teeny details—like cutting the video in just the right spot to get rid of the "umm, uhhh" before the good part of your speech. But you'll be able to add professional transitions, nice titles, extra graphics and background music without much hassle.

Ever have a nice clip for your business that needs a little polish? Try **BUZZcard,** a startup that lets you take your own logo to create an intro and end for your videos with the touch of a button or two. Just create your animations then upload your video. The system slaps the beginning and end on your project and lets you export it wherever you need. Unfortunately they increased their prices in June of 2013, but if you do a lot of videos, the $29.95/month is worth it.

YouTube does a great job of keeping up with the technology times and adding helpful features. The Video Editor is a great example. Rather than making you fuss with a downloaded editor to perfect your YouTube videos, the service lets you upload your clip and edit directly on the screen, for free, of course.

You can combine videos, both yours and others, in the Creative Commons domain. And you can add audio, transitions, text and special effects. Although the tools are not incredibly fancy, they allow you to smooth out rough edges on an online piece that represents you and your organization.

Multimedia Editors at a Glance

(recommended tools in **bold**)

Audacity	Downloadable, open-source audio editor	**Free**	**audacity.sourceforge.net**
BUZZcard	Online video editor that adds intro and closing animations	$29.95/month	buzzcard.com
Ezvid	Screen recorder, slideshow maker and video editor for Windows	Free	ezvid.com
iMovie	**Video editor for Macs and iOS devices**	**$14.99 for Mac, or $4.99 for iOS app**	**apple.com/ilife/imovie**
Windows Movie Maker	Free Microsoft video editor for Windows	Free	windows.microsoft.com/en-US/windows-live/movie-maker-get-started
YouTube Video Editor	Basic multimedia editor for YouTube videos	Free	youtube.com/editor

Color Pickers and Analyzers

Color Cop

Colorfy It

ColorSnapper

ColorZilla

Pixie

Your electronic and print collateral will look ever so much more awesome if you can customize colors and fonts to make everything look uniform. A number of teeny tiny tools can help you identify the colors in an image or file with a couple of clicks.

These tools range from drag-over pixel identifiers that pop up the codes to sites that will analyze images or whole websites for all the colors.

My favorite has always been **Pixie,** a tiny little program that allows you to identify colors on the screen so you can create graphics and documents that match. You can keep it running all the time or simply call upon it when you need it. The default is that it sits on top of your other programs all the time. I found this annoying, so I turned it on and off. But it'll show the codes for the color of a pixel so you can replicate a color scheme.

Color Cop is a reader favorite, drawing a couple of recommendations every time the subject comes up. I'm fond of **ColorZilla** for picking colors on the web, and I keep **ColorSnapper** on my Mac as a Pixie replacement. Every once in a while I throw a site into the **Colorfy It** analyzer to reveal the colors in a website.

Color Pickers and Analyzers at a Glance

(recommended tools in **bold**)

Color Cop	**Multifunctional color picker for Windows**	**Free**	colorcop.net
Colorfy It	Online website color analyzer	Free	colorfyit.com
ColorSnapper	Color picker for Macs	$4.99	colorsnapper.com
ColorZilla	**Web-based color tool for Chrome and Firefox that includes image analyzer**	**Free**	colorzilla.com
Pixie	**Simple color picker for Windows**	**Free**	nattyware.com/ pixie.php

Chapter 15

Presentations
and Surveys

W e humans are social creatures, always striving to both share information with and collect information from each other. This chapter
shares the piles and piles of tools that help us do both.

Surveys, forms and Polls

bizodo

Google Forms

Jotform

Poll Everywhere

Polldaddy

SurveyMonkey

Wufoo

I think it's safe to say that **SurveyMonkey** is the leader in the online survey field. The company was founded in 1999 and has dominated the market for quite some time, gobbling up rivals and related companies along the way, such as **Wufoo,** Zoomerang and Precision Polling.

SurveyMonkey has always had a pretty cool free version, although it's tightened the features over the years. These days, you get 10 questions per survey and up to 100 responses, but you can't download any of the data or do anything fancy such as branching based on answers or extensive data analysis.

If your organization really needs survey software, the upgrade versions of this tool are worth the prices (starting at $17/month). It has added some really cool data analysis features that allow you to break apart results to look at the data from all sides. The first time I used it for a major benchmarking survey for one of my clients, we had to pay an outside statistician the big bucks to pull the data apart to get to the real trends (OK, it was my dad, but he *is* a statistician). By the time we did the follow-up survey, SurveyMonkey had added so many rich analysis tools that my poor father was out of work.

Chapter 15 ~ Presentations and Surveys

SurveyMonkey has plenty of competitors, most of them with some type of free version, such as **bizodo's** 150 responses or 100 for **JotForm.** You'll find the capability to share on social media networks, apps or formatting to make the surveys tablet/mobile friendly and various integrations with other apps and services, such as email and e-commerce.

JotForm (which also spells its name "Jotform," driving a former English teacher like me crazy!) has a cool integration with Dropbox that deposits submissions directly into your cloud storage. Plus, it has this cool little feature called Wishbox that lets visitors to your website grab a screenshot of something that bugs them and draw arrows to the problem to show you what's wrong. JotForm has mobile apps and integrated e-commerce, too.

Although **Google Forms** lacks sophisticated analysis tools, it takes just minutes to build a simple survey that updates instantly into a Google Drive spreadsheet. Oh, and it's free for as many questions and responses as your heart desires and very handy for collecting responses on mobile devices.

Polldaddy comes from the makers of WordPress (Page 47), so the tool is easily integrated into blogs and other websites. You can collect responses online, via Twitter, the mobile app and other options. The free version is more generous than SurveyMonkey, giving you 200 responses and 10 questions per survey.

As for Wufoo, which is now a SurveyMonkey company, you have to give a second look to a service that named itself after the musical groups Wu-Tang Clan and the Foo Fighters. Wufoo helps you create contact forms, online surveys and invitations so you can collect the data, registrations and online payments you need without writing a single line of code. You can embed Wufoo forms into your site, and they integrate into other services such as MailChimp (Page 144) and Basecamp (Page 62).

Lastly but perhaps best-ly, we have **Poll Everywhere.** Poll Everywhere is a live polling site that allows attendees to respond to a survey with a tweet, text or online entry. You can create multiple-choice polls or use the brainstorming feature so attendees can share words or phrases live with the group.

I use Poll Everywhere all the time to engage attendees, asking fun questions such as, "How much of a nerd are you?" and "Who first coined the word 'nerd'?" People love seeing the results pop up in real time, and it breaks up a regular old lecture.

Regular audience-response systems cost thousands of dollars, but Poll Everywhere is more than reasonable. It's free for up to 40 responses per poll, and paid versions start at just $15/month.

Surveys, Forms and Polls at a Glance (recommended tools in **bold**)

bizodo	Online survey and form builder	Free for 3 forms and 150 submissions per month, or paid for up to 10 forms for $25/month	bizodo.com
Google Forms	**Free forms and surveys connected to Google spreadsheets**	**Free**	**forms.google.com**
JotForm	Online survey and form builder	Free for unlimited forms and 100 submissions per month, or paid levels starting at $9.95/month	jotform.com
Poll Everywhere	**Real-time audience response system and polling tool**	**Free for up to 40 responses per poll, or starting at $15/month**	**polleverywhere.com**

Surveys, Forms and Polls at a Glance (continued)

Polldaddy	Flexible, easy online polling site with iOS app from the makers of WordPress	Free for 10 questions and 200 responses, or starting at $29/month for many more features	polldaddy.com
SurveyMonkey	SurveyMonkey audience has hundreds of thousands of respondents ready and willing to give feedback.	Free for 10 questions and 100 responses, or starting at $17/month for yearly billing for many more features	surveymonkey.com
Wufoo	Online form and registration site	Free for 3 forms and 100 responses per month, or paid versions start $14.95/month	wufoo.com

Presentation Tools

Brainshark

Keynote

Prezi

SlideRocket

SlideShare

SlideShark

Slide-based presentation software gets a lot of bad publicity for being a boring and outdated tool for education (There's even a book called *Death by PowerPoint.*), but many speakers (myself included) still rely on the infamous slide deck to share key points during presentations. PowerPoint is still the industry standard, but we have a number of cool alternatives and related resources to make the boring presentation much more modern.

The first time I saw the anagram feature of a presentation made with **Keynote**, I knew I had to have it. The slide transition effect caused the letters on one slide to look like they were rearranging and transforming themselves into the words on the next slide.

I purchased it first for my mobile devices; and although they were full-featured versions, it was hard to create an entire presentation on a phone or tablet.

Thus—I'm almost ashamed to admit this—the opportunity to own Keynote and make my letters fly around was one of the top reasons I decided to switch from my PC to a Mac. Keynote is the strongest piece of Apple's iWork office suite. It has innovative animations and features that help your presentations shine—well worth the $20.

SlideRocket is an online presentation platform that lets you create, manage, share and measure the impact of your presentations. Watch a few of the presentation demos, and you'll see a whole host of cool special effects, professional touches and entertaining multimedia.

It's easy to use; and all your presentations are accessible online, meaning you no longer have to worry about whether you have the full version of PowerPoint on your computer. The free version is pretty robust, so you might not need to spend $240 a year for the bonus features. The mobile apps give you access to your presentations on the go.

I hate it when a company asks you to "contact us" for pricing; but at least **Brainshark** has a fun, free level to give the tool a try. This cool presentation tool lets you record audio via phone or computer for each slide, and the self-playing presentation sits in a frame with navigation tools and slide titles.

Brainshark's enterprise systems (the "contact us" level) includes a mobile viewer for presentations on the go; but its iOS app, **SlideShark,** earns a mention for an impressive tool for PowerPoint presentations, including the capability to turn your iPhone into a remote control for the presentation on your iPad and, at the paid levels, to keep a repository of presentations for a sales team.

Once you've created a presentation masterpiece, you can upload it to **SlideShare** for hosting, sharing and increasing your online web presence. SlideShare is an SEO bonanza, indexing the words in your uploaded documents and boosting your rank when it links back to (or is embedded in) your main site. LinkedIn purchased SlideShare in 2012, so now you can easily share your presentations and expertise-rich documents through LinkedIn.

The site's free version gives you plenty of extra SEO exposure; and, for another $19 a month, you can get analytics, integrate sales meetings and capture leads.

Now for something completely different. Think of **Prezi** as an endless whiteboard that you can use to tell a story. You put up images and words, and then you sweep a camera across the board, zooming in and out of points as you talk about them.

Instead of creating point-by-point slides, you illustrate your presentation with graphics, words and ideas. Then you use the tool to move from one point to the next, and the tool allows you to swirl in, pull out and do all kinds of special effects.

Prezi just keeps growing. In 2013, it is on track to welcome about 2 million new users per month. I haven't learned to love it yet for my presentations. Frankly, it makes me a little dizzy, but people adore it once they get used to the new format.

Another cool Prezi goodie—it has iOS mobile apps that let you both work on Prezi on the go and present using a touchscreen, which is perfect for the fluid format of the presentations.

NerdHerd Thumbs Up: Keynote

Janet S. McEwen is fond of the iOS version of Keynote that lets you edit your presentations on your mobile device.

Presentation Tools at a Glance

(recommended tools in **bold**)

Brainshark	Online presentations with your slides and recorded audio	Free for individual account, or "contact us" for enterprise brainshark.com	brainshark.com
Keynote	**Presentation software from Apple**	**$19.99**	**apple.com/ iwork/keynote**
Prezi	Innovative PowerPoint alternative	Free for public Prezis, or starting at $59/year for more options	prezi.com
SlideRocket	Online presentation creation software with free version	Free for basic features, or professional versions start at $24/month	sliderocket.com
SlideShare	**Presentation sharing site for PDFs, PowerPoints and other documents**	**Free with limits, or starting at $19/month for many more features**	**slideshare.net**
SlideShark	PowerPoint presentation player for iOS devices	Free for up to 100MB, or starting at $49/year for more features and storage	slideshark.com

This book is interactive!
Scan with the Layar App for
updates, bonus material and more

Magazine and Book Tools

Book Creator

CreateSpace

Google Currents

iBooks Author

Issuu

Scribd

Scrivener

Yudu Media

These days, it's surprisingly easy to publish your own book, magazine or extended brochure. Many of the self-publishing sites have been around for quite some time—Lulu is a well-known veteran with a great reputation. But for this book, I decided on **CreateSpace**, a print-on-demand service from Amazon.com.

Creating a book can be a wonderful marketing tool for small businesses, consultants, chambers of commerce and associations. For just a few dollars a book, you might:

✔ Publish a history of your organization

✔ Showcase your expertise

✔ Turn your blog into a book

✔ Create a guide to your city

✔ Enhance your sales portfolio

✔ Collect your white papers and reports

CreateSpace doesn't charge anything to upload a PDF, review it for errors, create a simple cover and publish. You can purchase lots of extras, including marketing packages, design help, extended distribution and more. It's fairly intuitive to use, and it pays royalties far above what you'd get with a regular publisher.

The biggest benefit, at least for small-volume publishers like myself who sell most books on-site, is that it charges very low prices for author's copies. And the turnaround once you order is a matter of days, where traditional publishing of my last book took—gulp—months and months.

CreateSpace can help you publish to Amazon's e-book store as well (Kindle), and you can convert your manuscript to the universal ePUB format to offer it on other digital bookstores.

Another major player in the e-book world is Apple; and it has shared free tools to produce books for its bookshelves, such as **iBooks Author** for the Mac. You can also download **Book Creator** on your iPad to create a book on your tablet. **Scrivener** is another Mac book-publishing program for simple layouts.

But a book or magazine doesn't have to be in printed form to make a splash. **Issuu** is one of those tools that can really make you look like a superstar. Have you ever created a fantastic PDF brochure or report—that no one read? Just upload your beautiful PDF to the mystical, magical Issuu site; and your boring document will be transformed into an interactive, dynamic, interesting online resource.

The site transforms almost any type of document into online magazines, books or catalogs that people can flip through. The graphics of the viewing interface will make you look like a pro, and it has built-in features that allow readers to share and download your files. I also like that you can create an Issuu mini version to embed into your site.

During the past year, it's added the capability to print your document straight from the site; and although the hard copies look great, it's quite expensive. It has also overhauled the settings to make sure your Issuu documents can be thumbed through on mobile devices.

Scribd is another site that allows uploading, analytics and indexing; and you can sell your work there as well. It makes its money from readers, so it's a free service for content providers. **Yudu Media** can also host your documents for sharing.

You'll be able to send links to your documents (private or public); and you can see usage analytics, including how many people looked at your document, what page they stopped looking and how many people downloaded it.

Google Currents is not really a magazine or book producer, but it's a cool way to curate and share your information on mobile sites. In a matter of minutes, you can hook up feeds from YouTube, your blog and other places that will feed the issue, which is available in the Google Currents app.

As far as I know, this app is not a huge success so far. A competitor to the awesome Flipboard content aggregator (Page 105), Currents lets you push your information in minutes in an interesting format. Since it's so easy to produce and free, I figure it's worth a shot.

Augmented Reality

Layar

If you create any printed material that other people read—I mean almost *anything* – you will love **Layar,** a free service and app (iOS and Android). Layar brings your printed material to life to the nth degree. In sum, it allows you to add links, information and multimedia to any document with amazing ease and at no cost. *Dwell* magazine and *Lonely Planet* travel guides are both using Layar to enhance their pages, and I foresee quite a future for the technology. You will, of course, need to tell your readers that the dynamic content is there and that they have to download Layar to see it, but it beats static old QR codes all to heck!

The applications of Layar are unlimited, but here are some ideas:

- ✔ Add additional details to your business card
- ✔ Distribute handouts to the conference via the brochure
- ✔ Send out postcards with a super-secret offer
- ✔ Print large volumes of a generic brochure and add specific or time-sensitive updates
- ✔ Give recipients easy ways to share your content or specials
- ✔ Increase your social media network with links to your Facebook and Twitter pages

Nerdy Tip: We're Layared!

We've embedded super-secret updates and goodies into this book using Layar. Just load the app and scan this graphic to see the awesome embedded extras.

This book is interactive!
Scan with the Layar App for
updates, bonus material and more

Magazine and Book Tools at a Glance (recommended tools in **bold**)

Book Creator	iPad app to create iBooks	$4.99	redjumper.net
CreateSpace	**Amazon.com's print-on-demand and self-publishing service**	**Free to create and upload, or receive professional help for various fees; expanded distribution or changes to original are both $25**	**createspace.com**
Google Currents	App-based magazine-type publisher for iOS and Android	Free	current.google.com
iBooks Author	Mac app that lets you create e-books from templates	Free	apple.com/ibooks-author

Magazine and Book Tools at a Glance (continued)

Issuu	Online service that turns PowerPoints and other documents into flippable catalog	Free for the ad-supported level, or $19/month for pro	issuu.com
Layar	Augmented reality tool	Free for ad-supported level, or paid plans for ad-free layars and enhanced SEO	layar.com
Scribd	Online magazine publishing site with e-commerce	Free	scribd.com
Scrivener	Mac and Windows download for writing and publishing books	$40 for Windows; $45 for Mac	literatureandlatte.com
Yudu Media	Online magazine publishing site	Free for basic, or more features such as embedded video and no ads start at about $160/year	free.yudu.com

SEO Alert!

Many of these tools that store evidence of your expertise can serve as keyword-building platforms to enhance your presence on the web. The documents you upload to Issuu and SlideShare are indexed by search engines just like the pages on your website. Make sure your slides and documents have great phrases and keywords so you can get found, and build link exchanges between the external sites and your web page.

Chapter 16

. . . .

Meeting Tools

In this chapter:

Technology is blurring the line between the tools for a monthly tele-conference with your board of directors and the platforms for host-ing a webinar for 200 attendees. These days, you can find free and low-cost tools that work for both. And before you figure out how you're going to get people together, you have to figure out when you'll meet and what you're hoping to accomplish. I love the free and bargain tools in this chapter that help you get organized and make meetings more productive.

Meeting Scheduling Tools

BookMe

Doodle

ScheduleOnce

WhenIsGood

Let's do some math:

You need to schedule a meeting with five attendees.

You send out one email to ask, "When can we meet?"

Each attendee sends you back a reply (x5).

You reply back to each (x5).

Then you send to the entire group (x1).

Each attendee writes back twice (x5x2).

When you add it all up, that's approximately one kabillion emails to schedule one 30-minute meeting.

There is an easier way!

The first time I found **Doodle,** I sighed with happiness. Without ever entering your email address or any personal information, you can pro-pose several dates and times for a meeting. Then Doodle generates a link for both your admin view and the participants' responses. You send the link to your participants, and everyone responds with availability, allowing you to use the admin view to find the perfect time.

I have used it for years, but recently it's upped its game to make it even more valuable. Now you can use the iOS apps ($2.99) to check on your schedules and propose more meetings. Plus it's added a new service called a MeetMe page that gives you a private URL you can send to colleagues to let them propose a time to meet based on your availability. For the advanced features, you need to register for a free account and connect your calendar. Premium Doodle (That sounds funny, doesn't it?) starts at $29/year.

It's also branched out into business scheduling with a service called **BookMe,** which lets you offer customers the capability to schedule their own appointments. BookMe is a little pricy, starting at $9/month for one user.

As awesome as Doodle has been for me over the years, I have a new love. **ScheduleOnce** is my new favorite meeting scheduling tool. I used to use **WhenIsGood,** which is very easy and very cool but not very attractive. ScheduleOnce couples the high-tech interface with easy-to-understand functionality.

Unlike Doodle, where you have to choose certain times and ask participants to pick, ScheduleOnce and WhenIsGood both let participants drag their mice over available blocks so the system can identify a common time when all participants can meet.

ScheduleOnce also has capabilities like Doodle's BookMe, with which you can send a web page to clients to ask them to pick their own appointment times.

NerdHerd Thumbs Up: Doodle

Renita Fonseca from the Texas Radiological Society uses Doodle weekly for scheduling weekly volleyball, ladies' night out, voting for board decisions, food ordering and more. "Doodle is a very versatile tool that has saved me HOURS of work!"

Meeting Agendas and Notes

Agreedo

Minutes.io

Just because you have a great way to conduct a meeting doesn't mean your meeting is going to be productive. But you can make use of a couple of free tools to keep you and your meeting organized, on track and effective.

Before meetings, you can use either **Agreedo** or **Minutes.io** to prepare agendas and enter attendees. During the meetings, just keep the sites open to take notes, record decisions, create action items and take attendance. After the meeting, you can email the meeting notes to the attendees and reiterate the action items.

Meeting Management at a Glance   (recommended tools in **bold**)

AgreeDo	Online meeting-management site and action item tracker	Free	agreedo.com
Book.Me	Appointment-setting site from Doodle	Free for basic, or $9/month for premium	doodle.com/bookme
Doodle	Simple meeting scheduling with no registration	Free for basic, or starting at $39/year for ad-free Premium solo level	doodle.com
Minutes.io	**Meeting-management tool with agenda, action items and note-taking capabilities**	**Free**	**minutes.io**
ScheduleOnce	**Meeting scheduling site with intuitive interface and easy controls, plus appointment-setting functionality**	**Free for group scheduling and MeetMe page, or starting at $5/month to integrate multiple calendars and remove ads**	**scheduleonce.com**
WhenIsGood	Simple meeting scheduling	Free	whenisgood.net

Audio Conferencing

FreeConferenceCall.com

Speek

UberConference

Who'da thunk that technology startups would seek to make tele-conferencing more fun? The new options for meeting with people via phone are very cool, indeed. Instead of using the traditional phone number and PIN code, the new systems connect with the web, smart devices and your computer with just a click of a button rather than a series of pound signs and access codes.

One shiny new tool is **Speek.** Go to its app or the site, and you're prompted to create a private URL for your teleconferences. Then send that link to your invitees, and they can connect through devices or computers. The system will even call out to participants at their desktops or dial a phone for them through a device.

On your Speek site, you can watch the interactions, mute and unmute callers, and invite more attendees. The Pro version ($10/month) also lets you drop files into the web interface to share with others. Speek even offers to create a Dropbox folder for your account that will save the shared documents.

UberConference is similar to Speek with a limit of five participants, but you can earn spots for up to 17 by spreading the word. When people call in, they show up on your own UberConference web page; and from there you can share files, record the session, and mute or unmute participants. When people speak, their icons (or pictures if they've hooked up their accounts) pop to the top of the screen.

If you pay for the UberConference pro version, the system will actually call participants for you at the appointed time. And iOS and Android apps let you take all the features on the go with you.

If you're not ready for web-based audio conferencing, there's always the reliable free conference call companies, such as the appropriately named **FreeConferenceCall.com.** I've long relied on sites such as FreeConference-Call.com for a free phone number and PIN that I can share for teleconferences. Up to 96 attendees can join in by dialing a regular old U.S. phone number. The attendees incur regular charges for making a long-distance call, and no one has to pay any extra. Because so many people have flat-rate plans for calling or lots of minutes through their business accounts, there's no need to feel guilty for not offering a toll-free number.

Video Conferencing

Google+ Hangouts

Meetings.io

ooVoo

Skype

Google+ Hangouts may change the way you conduct your meetings. Start your meeting in a matter of minutes by inviting colleagues to connect via their Google+ accounts (any Gmail account works). Each participant (up to 10) shows up in a video line below the main screen; and when people speak, they pop up to the main screen.

In addition, you can broadcast your Hangout live through your YouTube account. This is a great opportunity to invite members to watch a discussion of industry trends among invited experts. You can record your Hangout (it's automatic if you're broadcasting live) and share it via YouTube.

Another option for videoconferencing is **ooVoo,** which allows up to 12 video participants per meeting from almost any device. Some of the cool features are the capabilities to record and send video messages and upload the videos to YouTube. The service also hooks into Facebook to offer instant video calls with your friends.

I'm really hoping **Meetings.io** stays awesome—and free. Just visit the site and push a button, and you immediately have a link to a "room" to which you can send to up to four other participants for an instant video meeting, complete with screen and file sharing. Did you notice I didn't say "log in"? That's right—no registration necessary. And you can make your meetings public or private.

In the world of online calling and Voice Over Internet Protocol, **Skype** is royalty. The name came from a mash of "sky" and "peer-to-peer conversations." Skype is a free download that allows you to chat via text or talk directly to another Skype viewer using a microphone and/or webcam.

It's free for video calls between two Skype users; but if you want to hold a business videoconference among up to 10 people (no more than five for the best quality), one person needs to have a Premium account ($4.99/month with a yearly subscription).

Skype also allows people to quickly share files and collaborate. Many businesses (including my former company) conduct regular meetings via Skype or just use it to pop off quick questions to colleagues across the hall. In addition to the communication to other Skype users, Skype allows you to make low-cost calls to landlines and mobiles. And the mobile apps lets you take the free or bargain calls with you.

Audio and Video Conferencing at a Glance

(recommended tools in **bold**)

FreeConferenceCall.com	Free conference calling for up to 96	Free	freeconferencecall.com
Google+ Hangouts	**Videoconferencing for up to 10 and live meeting broadcasts**	**Free**	**google.com/+ learnmore/hangouts**
Meetings.io	Instant video conferencing for up to 5 people	Free	meetings.io
ooVoo	Videoconferencing for up to 12 through multiple devices	Free for ad-based videoconferencing; or $29.99/year for ad-free, screensharing and storage	oovoo.com
Skype	Phone and videoconferencing software with lots of extras	Free download and apps; calling packages start at $2.99/month, or Premium for group videoconferencing for $4.99/month	skype.com

Audio and Video Conferencing at a Glance (continued)

Speek	Free conference call service for up to 10	Free for 5 participants, or $10/ month for unlimited	speek.com
UberConference	Free web-based conference calling for up to 17 attendees	Free for 5 participants, with chance to earn up to 17; $10/month for full version	uberconference.com

Live-Streaming Video Tools

Bambuser

Justin.tv

Livestream

Ustream

For my modest live-streaming video needs, Google+ Hangouts (Page 211) more than suffices, but if you'd like to share your live events with others, you have several options.

Ustream is probably the biggest live streaming service, and the site is full with magazine-style live broadcasts with professional effects and lots of viewership. For those of us with more modest live-streaming aspirations, you'll find Ustream an easy way to instantly broadcast from your computer or mobile device. Ustream free and paid apps will help you clean up your broadcasts. The free version is supported by ads, and paid versions start at $99/month.

Livestream has an ad-less free level, followed by a basic level for $42/month with a yearly subscription. The drawback with the free version is that your audience members have to log in to Livestream to see you.

Bambuser and **Justin.tv** are two other live-streaming options, but neither has the traffic of Ustream or Livestream. But all four have free versions and the capability to broadcast from anywhere, so you can choose the interface you like the best.

Streaming Video at a Glance   (recommended tools in **bold**)

Bambuser	Live-streaming service with compatibility with hundreds of smartphones	Free, or paid plans start at $99/month with year commitment	bambuser.com
Justin.tv	Live-streaming site for computer-based broadcasts	Free with ads, or paid broadcasting plans starting at $99/month	justin.tv
Livestream	Ad-free live video streaming	Free, or paid plans starting at $42/month for year subscription	livestream.com
Ustream	**Live-streaming service with extensive audience**	**Free, or ad-free paid plans start at $99/month for year commitment**	**ustream.tv**

Screensharing Tools

Anymeeting

FreeScreenSharing

GoToMeeting

join.me

WebEx

If you find you need more than just a call or even a video chat for your meeting, you can find many tools that let you share screens and work together online with a few people or many.

GoToMeeting and **WebEx** are two of the biggest names in the web meeting/ webinar category, and they are both about $50/ month for the 25-attendee level. (WebEx also has a free version for up to three attendees, which is why it made the "At a Glance" list.) That pricing can be a little steep for smaller organizations, even if they have to have regular meetings, but we're lucky to have lots of lower-cost options with comparable functionality.

One of my favorites is **AnyMeeting,** which lets you share your screen with up to 200 people for free, with session recordings, audio (phone or online) and other amazing features with its basic plan. And if you sell tickets to your event (integrated into the registration system), AnyMeeting takes a small portion and upgrades you to the ad-free version.

AnyMeeting is also a great choice if your presentation includes video because it allows you to play a YouTube video that runs locally on each attendee's connection rather than through the streaming presentation (which makes it looks like a French Impressionist painting). The best feature about this free tool is that it allows you to schedule the events in advance, as opposed to my second-favorite free screensharing tool, **join.me.**

The very trustworthy company LogMeIn owns join.me. You don't even have to register to share your screen—just click the share button, download a little something-something and start sharing. The free version is great for instant meetings, especially when you find yourself saying, "Let's look at that screen together." You can invite up to 10 people to your event, and you can give screen control to another presenter. It includes a free conference call number and code, and you can also communicate through the interactive chat. It works on all common browsers and platforms.

There are plenty of other plans and programs out there, including **Free-ScreenSharing** from the makers of FreeConferenceCall.com. Google+ Hangouts (Page 211) are also awesome places to share your screen with a small group or broadcast it live via YouTube.

NerdHerd Thumbs Up: join.me

Kathy Benton from the Society for College and University Planning uses join.me extensively for volunteer training. She likes that the programs allows a co-presenter to control the screen.

Screensharing Tools at a Glance (recommended tools in **bold**)

AnyMeeting	**Screensharing and webinar tool for up to 200 participants, plus videoconferencing for up to 6**	**Free for basic up to 200 attendees, ad-free starts at $17.99/month for 25 attendees**	**anymeeting.com**
FreeScreen Sharing	Free screensharing for up to 96	Free	freescreensharing.com
join.me	Instant screensharing for up to 10 from the makers of LogMeIn	Free for basic, or meeting scheduling and other advanced features starting at $13/month for year subscription	join.me
WebEx	Free screensharing for up to 3 attendees	Free for 3 attendees, or starting at $24/month	webex.com

Whiteboards

BaiBoard

Twiddla

Vyew

Let's say you're designing a new website with a committee, and you guys need to work together to find the right look. **Twiddla** is the perfect tool. Without registering or downloading anything, you can push a button, share a link and immediately be on the same page with as many people as you want. You can mark up a document or webpage together, share notes, and talk online with integrated audio. The basic version, which is quite awesome and does most of the things that most of us will ever need, is free.

Twiddla isn't a screensharing site—you're simply both seeing the same document or page and marking it up. You also can't edit a document together, although you can write together with Etherpad. It won't work on Flash or secure sites. You also can't save your work if you have a free guest account, but you can always use Jing (Page 80) to save a screenshot.

Vyew has many of the features of Twiddla but goes even further. As with Twiddla, you can share documents, sites and blank pages to mark up and review. But with Vyew, you can also share your desktop and even take a screenshot to mark up. I also like the feature that allows you to add text and voice notes to a collaboration, and you can even reply to notes by others.

You can filter the collaborative pages by commenter to ensure that you can implement the suggestions that your board president gave you and ignore the dimwit on the team. (Note: If they're the same person, you're out of luck.) Vyew also allows audio and video conferencing and lets you share your work, even in the free version.

Vyew's ad-supported free version allows up to 10 collaborators, and paid versions start at about $10 a month.

If you need whiteboard-type collaboration functionality with a mobile team, **BaiBoard** might just work. The tool allows you to collaborate in real time with participants on computers and tablets. Right now, it's just available for Macs and the iPad; but Android functionality is coming. If you're simply showing a presentation to a group, you can show your iPad screen on any browser with the same Wi-Fi connection. BaiBoard is also convenient for PDF annotations and signatures.

Whiteboards at a Glance

(recommended tools in **bold**)

BaiBoard	Tablet-based whiteboard and collaboration tool	Free	baiboard.com
Twiddla	Online collaboration tool for brainstorming and co-browsing	Free, or paid plans with the capability to save documents at $14/month	twiddla.com
Vyew	**Online meeting rooms for real-time collaboration**	**Free for up to 10 participants, or paid plans start at $6.95/ month for year commitment**	**vyew.com**

This book is interactive!
Scan with the Layar App for
updates, bonus material and more

Guest Nerd: Five Most Essential Awesomeness Tools for Chambers from Frank J. Kenny

CRM

Facebook Groups

Facebook Lists

Nimble

Twitter lists

Focus x Relationship Building = Success

If you run a local chamber or similar small business and you want to get results through social media, this group of tools is for you. The idea behind these specific tools is creating awareness, relationships and sales.

Start with **Facebook.** Facebook is perfect for local organizations because Facebook is all about people you know, like and trust. Create a Facebook List of your members and prospects. Follow them, engage with them. Next, create a **Facebook group** and invite your members. Nurture it. Create a sense of community, not built around advertising and selling, but around relationships. Next, create a **Twitter list** with all of your members and prospects. Engage with them. Retweet their posts. Mention them in your tweets. All of this will create awareness and build relationships with your target market.

Use a CRM in the cloud, such as **ChamberMaster, Weblink** or **YourMembership** to manage the back end of your organization. Export that management data to **Nimble.** In Nimble, you manage the relationships that came from Facebook, Twitter and your CRM. Managed relationships lead to sales. You still have to ask for the sale. People say yes to those they know, like and trust.

Chamber Tools at a Glance

CRM	Any of the "in the cloud" back-office systems that help keep track of members, customers, accounting and events	From $129 up	chambermaster.com weblinkinternational.com yourmembership.com
Facebook Groups	Create an online area where your members (and maybe your prospects) can engage and build relationships.	Free	facebook.com/about/groups
Facebook Lists	Organize your members, customers or prospects in handy lists you can follow.	Free	facebook.com/addlist
Nimble	A social relationship management tool that pulls it all together for you, leading to sales. This is where you create and manage and grow the "know, like and trust."	$15/month	nimble.com
Twitter Lists	An easy way to group all of your members and prospects in one place so you can engage with them.	Free	twitter.com/lists

Frank J. Kenny is a speaker, writer and consultant. He is a leading authority on social media and technology for chambers, business associations and their members. As a faculty member for the U.S. Chamber of Commerce Institute for Organization Management, Frank instructs on Integrating Strategic Technology Solutions, Technology Tools and Trends and Using Data to Grow and Sustain Your Organization. Frank is the author of two books on social media and technology. Find him at FrankJKenny.com.

Chapter 17

. . . .

Online Event Management

Whether you're hosting a movie night for 20 or a charity gala for 200, you can take advantage of a whole pile of services that help you organize, promote and profit from your event.

Online event management is another crowded category of tech tools, and it can be tough to identify the best provider in the pack. In general, you can find tools that will:

- ✔ Charge small fees per ticket (usually less than $1/ticket plus a small percentage) as well as separate credit card processing fees

- ✔ Offer a maximum charge per ticket, no matter what the price (usually less than $10)

- ✔ Accept online and offline payments

- ✔ Waive all fees for free events

- ✔ Provide templates and guidance to set up an event homepage

- ✔ Allow custom registration forms so you can collect information you need for a successful event

- ✔ Integrate promotion tools, such as social media sharing and email blasts

- ✔ Provide registration lists and check-in tools for event day, including mobile ticket scanning

- ✔ Create online, printable tickets

- ✔ Schedule reminder emails and other communication for attendees

- ✔ Let you set up discount codes

- ✔ Offer private or public event settings

Online Event Management

Brown Paper Tickets

Event Farm

Eventbee

Eventbrite

EventSpot

Eventzilla

Guestlist

Some online event management tools stand out above the rest. My longtime favorite is **Eventbrite**, which I respect not only for its longevity but also for its long list of integrations and its continuing evolution. One of the best integrations is the capability to push your event into Facebook, which gives you another layer of promotion opportunities. In addition, Eventbrite is the chosen event planning app for another of my favorite tools, Paperless Post (Page 147), which sends beautiful, unusual email invitations to invitees. MailChimp (Page 144) is also a partner, meaning your invitations can be scooped up through its email blast system, which should be familiar to your database.

Another feature I like about Eventbrite is its At the Door app. You can use its card swiper with your iPad to collect cash and credit cards at the door for no service fee and just a 3 percent credit card processing charge. **Eventbee** and **Eventzilla** have similar features and various pricing levels.

I've seen some sneaky groups (like my former networking group) circumvent ticket fees by collecting money outside the event management system; but I think that's kind of a dirty trick, except perhaps if you're raising money for charity (or try **Guestlist** for free charity events). These services provide lots of features, and the small fees help keep them going.

If you manage a lot of events, you might try Constant Contact's integrated event management system, **EventSpot,** with flat-rate pricing per month rather than per-ticket fees. You'll still have to pay the PayPal commissions; and, of course, you must be a Constant Contact email customer (pricing starts at about $15/month).

As much as I like Eventbrite, **Brown Paper Tickets** is impressive. The fees (3.5 percent plus 99 cents) end up on the buyer side, so you end up with every penny of your ticket price. And if you use your own credit card processor, Brown Paper Tickets throws back some of its commission to offset the costs. Brown Paper Tickets also integrates into both MailChimp and Facebook Events.

But the coolest feature is its ticket printing service. It doesn't charge a dime to print and send hard-copy tickets to your attendees—what a nice touch! In addition, Brown Paper Tickets can sell your tickets at its own walk-up venues, although the list isn't very long. It also lets you buy pre-printed tickets to sell at the door.

If you have a guest list and are just looking to check people into an event, try **Event Farm,** an iOS app that lets you monitor attendance and even print badges with QR codes to ease registration. I also like that you can flag certain attendees to know when your VIPs arrive.

Online Event Management Tools at a Glance

(recommended tools in **bold**)

Brown Paper Tickets	**Online event management site with free ticket printing and shipping**	**Free for free events, or 3.5% plus 99¢/ticket with no additional credit card fees**	**brownpapertickets.com**
Event Farm	**Mobile check-in system for events (iOS only)**	**Check-in feature is free for first 100 attendees then 50¢/ guest**	**eventfarm.com**
Eventbee	Online event management tool with $1 flat fee pricing	Free for free events, or starting at $1 plus credit card fees	eventbee.com
Eventbrite	**Online event management tool**	**Free for free events, or 2.5% of the price plus 99¢/ticket, plus another 3% for credit card processing**	**eventbrite.com**
EventSpot	Constant Contact's event management service	$20-$25/month plus PayPal commissions	constantcontact.com/ eventspot
Eventzilla	Online event management tool with $1 flat-fee pricing	Free for free events, or $1 plus credit card fees per attendee	eventzilla.net
Guestlist	Online event registration and ticket sales	Free for free and charity events, or 2% commission and PayPal fees	guestlistapp.com

Casual Events

If you're planning a more casual event, you have plenty of options. **Evite** is one of the classics. An ad-based service, Evite lets you create a simple party page, send out invitations individually or through social media and track RSVPs. It's added some money-making tools lately, including gifts and an online invitation service called **Evite Postmark,** which competes directly with Paperless Post (Page 147).

Evite

InviteKix

Meetup

Punchbowl

Yapp

Zokos

Punchbowl is a cross between Evite and Paperless Post. You can also create a simple party site through Facebook Events. It's also free and has the built-in advantage of letting you publicize the events through one of the most popular social media sites. **Meetup.com** is another classic for casual events and groups, though it's best for recurring meetings. It's $12 a month to be a Meetup organizer but free to join, and many of the groups are free.

Zokos' events are made for chip-in parties, such as when you're collecting funds for a group dinner. You create an event and a goal for the minimum number of guests, and, like Kickstarter, no one is charged until the group makes the goal. Another Kickstarter (Page 253) similarity is that Zokos takes a fee from the contributions to process credit cards and pay for the service.

We're starting to see more and more drag-and-drop app builders, but this simple tool might hit the spot for a small, personal event. In about the time it would take you to set up an Evite, you can choose a theme in **Yapp,** fill in the event details, upload a picture or two, and invite your guests to download it. The app allows you to instantly share pictures and updates, keep up with Twitter feeds, map locations and keep all the pertinent details handy. Your new app can be pushed to Android and iOS app stores immediately and can be updated in minutes. And yep, Yapp is free.

InviteKix, a new offering in this category, is both oddly compelling and a smidge disturbing. InviteKix generates custom videos for your invitations. The video templates range from racy (Suzy Surprise) to amusing (Roamin' Roman) to completely creepy (Sensitive Steve and several others). It's free in beta, but you can only invite 10 people. It's definitely not appropriate for all audiences, but it'll amuse you. Kind of (shudder).

Casual Event Tools at a Glance

(recommended tools in **bold**)

Evite	**Party and event planning site**	**Free**	**evite.com**
InviteKix	Bizarre video invitation site for casual events	Free in beta	invitekix.com
Meetup	Casual event and group organization site	Free to join, or starting at $12/month to organize	meetup.com
Punchbowl	Cross between Evite and Paperless Post	Ad-supported free version, or paid versions start at $19/year	punchbowl.com
Yapp	Simple, do-it-yourself app creator for event	Free	yapp.us
Zokos	Event-planning site with crowdsourced funding options	Free to set up, then 3% commission and 30¢ for each guest	zokos.com

Volunteer Management

SignUpGenius **VolunteerSpot**	**VolunteerSpot** and **SignUpGenius** are two sites that help you organize help, resources and donations for an event. Both let you invite and track volunteers for an event, plus keep track of tasks, contributions and other event details.

VolunteerSpot also has a cool tablet app called Clipboard so you can manage signups and volunteer activities on-site.

Both sites are free for robust capabilities that will take care of the needs of most organizers, but you can upgrade to manage more complex events or to have an ad-free environment.

Volunteer Management Tools at a Glance
(recommended tools in **bold**)

SignUpGenius	Volunteer organization and sign-up sheets	Free for most features, or starting at $1.99/ month for ad-free sites	signupgenius.com
VolunteerSpot	Volunteer organization and sign-up sheets	Free for most features, or starting at $4.99/month for more complex events and needs	volunteerspot.com

Behind the Glasses:
Build Your Own Photo Booth

Grab your fake mustaches and big straw hats—you need a photo booth at your next event! These days, photo booths at events are so popular that you can find dozens of photo booth providers willing to bring their equipment to your events for a few hundred dollars, but you can also create your own with $60 and a computer.

When I decided to put together a Nerdy Photo Booth for my presentations, I researched at least a dozen software packages from free to hundreds of dollars. My favorite is **Sparkbooth,** a fairly inexpensive program for Mac and Windows computers.

The reason Sparkbooth stood out among the rest is the capability to personalize the photo templates so you can brand your company and event. I also like that it integrates with my MailChimp account, meaning that people who sign up to receive their photos will receive an invitation to opt in to my newsletter, NerdWords. It took me a while to personalize all the features and create the template, but now I can have the program up and running at any photo-worthy moment.

Since installing Sparkbooth, I've come up with lots of reasons to use it, including a friend's Sweet 16 party. I even used it as a fundraiser at a 5k race, running the computer on battery power in a park to capture happy race finishers and later asking for donations when I sent them their photos. For the most part, I don't print the photo booth pictures, choosing instead to automatically upload them to a Dropbox folder and sharing that link with groups, so they can find and download their own pictures while enjoying other smile-filled photos.

Tips for a Great Photo Booth

- ✔ Lighting is critical.

- ✔ Make sure you have adequate ambient lighting, or invest in a USB-powered light for your computer.

- ✔ People love props.

- ✔ I carry my Hello Kitty "I Love Nerds" lunchbox filled with nerdy glasses to every event, and attendees love to dig through the box to find the most outrageous accessories to make themselves smile. Bring a box of silly hats, feather boas and other fun goodies to spice up your pictures.

- ✔ Watch the per-picture timing.

- ✔ Sparkbooth has templates with one to four pictures, but you want to make sure you choose an option that helps people move in and out of your booth area in a timely manner so you don't end up with a line. Ditto with your post-picture processing. If you are going to have people add contact information, include the minimum number of fields possible and set the timer so people don't dally.

Chapter 18

Travel Tools

Even if you travel only once a year, you can save time, money and hassle by taking advantage of a wide range of travel tools and apps, most of which are free. They're designed to help you keep organized, stay informed, zero in on things you need on the road and keep you sane.

Commuting Tools

Gasbuddy

Moovit

Waze

When Apple and Google were fighting over the No. 1 spot for mobile map apps, **Waze** drove up and charmed us all. Like the other two navigation tools, Waze offers turn-by-turn navigation to get you where you want to go; but instead of relying on a database of maps and official traffic reports, Waze lets its members report real-time delays, speed traps, accidents and other road hazards.

If I had someplace to commute to, I'd use Waze every day. When you program in your home and work, the community of users will help you avoid traffic and trouble. Waze encourages chattiness and helpfulness with a point system, plus it connects with your social networks to let you and your friends keep tabs on one another; and now that it's part of the Google empire, look for even more integrations and connections. I like the feature that allows you to send anyone a trackable update on your ETA. Of course, if you're at the cupcake store and don't want anyone to know, you should turn this feature off.

Like **Gasbuddy,** Waze helps you find the lowest prices on gas in your area, with data available from other members as well as Yelp and FourSquare. And the service also lets you collect coupons and specials from participating merchants during your travels.

If you're looking for a Waze-type guide for public transportation, **Moovit** is an international resource for real-time updates from fellow passengers. In 2013, Moovit is available in select cities in about a dozen countries and growing.

Ground Transportation

Taxi Magic
TaxiFareFinder
TaxiFinder

Trying to decide whether you should take the shuttle or spring for a cab? Visit **TaxiFare-Finder** to get an idea of how much a taxi ride would be. I've used it several times; and I've found it to be quite accurate, even taking into account differences in local taxi rates.

I hesitate a little to recommend a popular transportation app called **Taxi Magic**. The concept is great: cab companies register with Taxi Magic; and when you order a taxi via your app, one of them will pick up the request, accept your online payment and come get you. But I've heard stories of cab no-shows, money mishaps and general discontentedness. But it's worth trying, and I'm optimistic that it'll work out the bugs. TaxiFare-Finder also offers its **TaxiFinder** iOS app, which helps you estimate taxi fares on the go plus find and call a taxi wherever you are.

Sharing Economy Services

Airbnb
Lyft
RelayRides
SideCar
Uber

Airbnb, Lyft, SideCar and **RelayRides** represent a new category of travel tools—the "sharing economy." The services make their money by connecting people who have rooms or transportation that they aren't using with people who need a ride or a place to stay.

Airbnb is a peer-to-peer marketplace for lodging, everything from a night or two in a loft in New York City to a beachside condo for a month in the Florida Keys. RelayRides lets people rent its cars to other RelayRides members. Lyft and SideCar hook up drivers and riders for rideshare opportunities. Riders and drivers work out a "donation" (not a "fee" or "fare," mind you), and the services subtract 20 percent of the donation for their own coffers.

The sharing economy is an interesting trend to watch because of the legal challenges. Some cities are accusing Airbnb members of running illegal hotels. Lyft and SideCar are in trouble with the California agency that regulates taxi and limo services because it considers them passenger carriers and wants them to carry commercial-level insurance and liability policies. SideCar sued the city of Austin for banning ridesharing app services in the city. RelayRides carries a million-dollar policy for its members, but a member's fatal crash that caused injuries that may exceed the insurance exposed the gray area of liability for peer-to-peer rentals.

Legal issues aside, these services offer cost-effective (and super cool) alternatives to the standard travel experience. A hotel in San Francisco can cost hundreds, but you can find Airbnb rooms for less than $100. And it's way cooler to rent a Lamborghini in Southern California than a Honda Civic. It'll be interesting to see the legal and regulatory issues shake out as we embrace the new sharing economy.

Uber is like Taxi Magic (Page 233) but with fancy car and limo services instead of taxis. They are more expensive than taxis, but users love the capability to summon a nice car to get where they need to go. You don't even have to download the app—just text your address and someone will come get you. It recently expanded UBERx, its lower-cost alternative that puts it directly into competition with Lyft and SideCar. Like the other sharing-economy startups, Uber is fighting legal battles; but it continues to expand in the United States and beyond.

Ground Transportation and Sharing Economy Tools at a Glance

(recommended tools in **bold**)

Airbnb	**Peer-to-peer lodging rental community**	**Varies**	**airbnb.com**
GasBuddy	Online and mobile resource to find the lowest gas prices	Free	gasbuddy.com
Lyft	Peer-to-peer ridesharing app	Varies	lyft.me
Moovit	Real-time monitoring and updates for public transportation on iOS and Android devices	Free	moovitapp.com
RelayRides	Peer-to-peer vehicle rentals	Varies	relayrides.com
SideCar	Peer-to-peer ridesharing service	Varies	side.cr
Taxi Magic	Mobile app to order, track and pay for taxis	Free	taximagic.com
TaxiFare Finder	**Taxi fare estimations**	**Free**	**taxifarefinder.com**
TaxiFinder	Taxi finding iOS app with directories from TaxiFareFinder	Free	taxifinder.com
Uber	Private car transportation service and ridesharing	Varies	uber.com
Waze	**Community-driven navigation app for commuting and travel**	**Free**	**waze.com**

Translation Tools

Bing Translator

Google Translate

Word Lens

Word Lens is just plain fun, even if you're not traveling. Download the app on your iOS or Android device, and hold the viewfinder over any printed material (headlines and sign-like formats work best). The printed words will transform into another language in front of your eyes, like a secret decoder ring—even if you're not connected to the Internet, which is awesome if you're trying to avoid international data roaming charges.

The bummer thing is the price, but relatively speaking, $5 isn't a lot of money to have an instant sign translator for your trip to Mexico. Besides Spanish/English, you can also purchase French, Italian and German language packs, with more to come. But if you're a lucky Windows phone owner, you can use **Bing Translator** with even more languages for free.

Another great translation tool is **Google Translate.** The website lets you type any phrase, and it instantly translates to whatever language you choose in real time, then you can save the translations into a virtual Phrasebook. The app is even cooler, allowing you to speak your phrase for a translation, then play back the phrase in the second language. This tool would have come in really handy when I was lost in Paris during my high school trip, struggling to understand enough French to get back to the hotel.

Review Sites

Trip Advisor **Yelp**	My favorite review sites for travel are **Trip Advisor** for hotels and **Yelp** for local recommendations for restaurants so I don't have to eat the hotel café's version of the ubiquitous lemon chicken with capers dish. Although both sites have faced alle-

gations of phony reviews, they offer the most robust and enthusiastic communities; and each time I've visited, I've found helpful advice that led me in the best directions.

The Yelp app is particularly helpful on the road. Yelp will let you filter by restaurants within walking distance that are open, and if you're in a fairly populated area, look through the Yelp Monocle viewfinder to see reviews of every business around you pop up and float in the air over their front doors.

Yeah. Cool.

Bonus Travel Tools

Minimus **STAYConnect**	Ewwww. I get grossed out when I think about the studies that show how many germs and other gross things collect on hotel remote con- trols. That's why I am thrilled when I turn on a TV and see the **STAYConnect** app option.

After you download the app to your device, you connect it to your hotel TV with a code to turn your device into a remote. For a small surcharge, you have access to a TV guide so you can see what's on and touch your screen to go the channel, rather than scrolling through every channel. You can also preview pay-per-view programs, read about local attractions and even check out of the hotel—all with your phone or tablet. And the only germs you have to worry about are yours.

Minimus isn't free or even high tech, but it's handy for travelers who need tiny versions of their favorite personal and household products to take on the road, from fancy organic brands to super-cheap soap slivers. The site has more than 2,000 super-small products at very reasonable prices (tiny toothpastes for less than a buck). It even offers free shipping if you spend $20 or more.

On-the-Road Help at a Glance   (recommended tools in **bold**)

Bing Translator	Free translation service for written and spoken words for Windows devices	Free	bing.com/translator
Google Translate	Free online and mobile translations for dozens of languages for both written and spoken words	Free	translate.google.com
Minimus	Online store dedicated to travel-size and miniature products	Varies	minimus.biz
STAYConnect	**Mobile app that turns iOS and Android devices into hotel TV remote controls**	**Free**	**Available in Apple and Google app stores**
TripAdvisor	Reviews of hotels, flights and vacation rentals	Free	tripadvisor.com
Word Lens	**Android and iOS translation app for signs and written material**	**Free for app, plus $4.99/ language pack**	**questvisual.com**
Yelp	**Local review site for restaurants, stores and services**	**Free**	**yelp.com**

Trip Organization Tools

	TripIt is a wow-oh-wow tool, a life-changing tool,
TripIt	an I-can't-believe-I-ever-left-home-without-it tool.
WorldMate	The concept is simple—just forward all your travel

TripIt is a wow-oh-wow tool, a life-changing tool, an I-can't-believe-I-ever-left-home-without-it tool. The concept is simple—just forward all your travel confirmations to plans@tripit.com, which is connected to the email address you use to forward. TripIt absorbs your confirmation and makes all the plans available on your mobile device.

Let's say you're planning a trip to Chicago in May. In January, you book the airfare and forward the confirmation. You find the perfect hotel room in April, and you snag a great deal on a rental car the day before you leave. TripIt has been using your forwarded confirmations to organize your trip behind the scenes; and when you head to the airport for your flight to Chicago, you open TripIt on your smartphone and open the trip that the app has named "Chicago, May 2014." Inside, you'll find your flight information, your hotel check-in time and confirmation number, the location of the rental car counter, and even the weather report for your stay. No more digging in your bag to find the confirmation you printed out to tell the taxi driver what hotel you're going to, or searching your email to figure out what time you have to get up to come home. The first time you use it, TripIt will prove itself to be an essential travel tool.

WorldMate is a worthy—perhaps superior—TripIt competitor. You don't have to forward your confirmations to WorldMate—it searches automatically. (So does TripIt for Gmail inboxes, but I found this service to be unreliable and buggy.) Both services are available on a wide range of mobile platforms, and they run neck-and-neck with their feature lists for the paid versions; but WorldMate's free version includes goodies such as a currency exchange calculator (so you don't have to use a separate one like XE Currency apps). And then there's the price. TripIt Pro is $49/year, and WorldMate Gold is $9.99.

Flight Tracking Tools

Expertflyer

Flight Status

Flight Update Pro

FlightAware

FlightView

GateGuru

Planely

SeatGuru

TravelNerd

I usually use the **FlightAware** site to look up my flights before I leave for the airport or to see where the delays are in airports around the country. But based on the app ratings, the services offered by **FlightView** might be a better choice. Both sites and their accompanying apps (for multiple mobile platforms) will let you see real-time updates on flights, delays and other travel situations that may cause you headaches. The FlightAware app is free, but the ads are annoying. FlightView has three versions, ranging from free to $3.99.

Some services integrate with TripIt, but they have their drawbacks. The nickel-and-dime charges with **Flight Status** are ridiculous, and **Flight Update Pro** (iOS only, $9.99) hasn't had an update since 2011. Sure, it won awards in 2010, but that's a lifetime ago in tech time!

How could you not love a site called **TravelNerd?** It's the best place to go to find an affordable airport parking lot—it even shares coupons. Plus, the site offers helpful facts about your airports, such as whether it offers free Wi-Fi or has family-friendly bathrooms.

GateGuru is another helpful tool for air travel. Before you leave for the airport, the free app tells you how long the security line wait might be and whether your flight is delayed. More importantly, when you're there, you can read reviews of the stores, services and restaurants in your terminal. I called upon it to find one of those ridiculous vibrating massage chairs one day when my back was killing me after a full day of travel. The chair didn't help that much, but I was grateful to the app for helping me find the only relief available.

SeatGuru is your insider view into the best seat in the house, or the plane, as it were. Just look up your flight on the site or the apps, and you'll find a blueprint of the plane with recommendations about where to sit and the seats to avoid. If you book later and end up stuck in a middle seat, sign up for the free version of **ExpertFlyer** to receive notifications when a better seat opens up.

Want company on your flight? Connect your social networks with TripIt and **Planely**, and you'll receive alerts when your contacts are traveling your way.

This book is interactive!
Scan with the Layar App for
updates, bonus material and more

Flight Tools at a Glance

(recommended tools in **bold**)

Tool	Description	Price	Website
ExpertFlyer	Travel help for better seats and reservations	Free for Seat Alert, or starting at $4.99/month for more travel help	expertflyer.com
Flight Status	Flight-tracking app with TripIt integration (for a fee)	$4.99 and up, plus extra charges for other services	flightstatus.us
Flight Update Pro	2011 flight-tracking app with TripIt integration	Starting at $4.99	silverwaresoftware.com/flight_update.html
FlightAware	**Flight-tracking site and apps**	**Free**	**flightaware.com**
FlightView	Mobile apps and online service for flight tracking	Free to $3.99	flightview.com
GateGuru	**Mobile airport guide with reviews, wait times and flight updates**	**Free**	**gateguruapp.com**
Planely	TripIt integration that lets you find social media connections when you travel	Free	planely.com
SeatGuru	**Maps and guides to help you find the best seat on the airplane**	**Free**	**seatguru.com**
TravelNerd	Airport parking rate resource with an awesome name	Free	travelnerd.com
TripIt	**Travel itinerary organizer**	**Free for basic, or $49/year for Pro**	**tripit.com**
WorldMate	Travel organizer and companion	Free app with lots of features, or $9.99 for Gold app	worldmate.com

Chapter 19

· ·

Outside Help

243

I saved this chapter for last because if you've read this whole book, you have way too many ideas about projects you want to accomplish and cool things you want to do. We'd all like to think we can live in that Enjoli perfume commercial from the '80s—the one that told us we should be able to bring home the bacon, fry it up then easily manage all the rest of our lives because we're empowered, enabled and incredible.

But one of the worst mistakes we make as professionals is that we try to do it all. If we own our own small businesses, we think we have to be the accountant, the marketer, the human resources department, the errand runner, and, of course, the chief cook and bottle washer. If we work in a small office, we assume that the more tasks we do ourselves, the more valuable we will seem to our employers.

Besides the superperson theory of overworking to get ahead, we all worry about the budget. How in the world would we ever have a budget to hire outside help?

I've been working for myself since 2007, first as a copywriter and now as a professional speaker. And I credit the following exercise with transforming my small businesses from overwhelming and exhausting to successful and enjoyable.

How to Determine if You Need Help

1. Write down every single task that you do at your job today.

2. Write down everything you would love to have the time to do to make your job better.

3. Review all your old task lists (and unfinished New Year's Resolutions). Then write down everything you should have done.

4. Look at the whole list, and star the things that *only* you can do.

5. Consider the unstarred items and estimate how many hours you spend taking care of things that other people could do. Chances are some of those tasks are things you don't like to do, and they may even be things that you are really bad at doing.

6. Circle those tasks, and imagine your job without those pains in the rear. How many hours a week are you spending on things that you hate, that other people are better at, just so you can save money and prove you can do it all?

I used to spend hours and hours on the weekends building websites, doing web research, stuffing envelopes for marketing mailings—all tasks I hated that took me forever. Then a few years ago, I realized that if I pawned off some of these jobs, I would be happier and more efficient.

My new rule of thumb for any new project is to weigh my expertise level and my time available with the number of hours it will take to do the task well. And if my nose crunches up at the thought of doing it myself, I hit one of the many, many communities of experts who can help.

The timing couldn't be better to give outsourcing a try. There are a whole host of completely awesome freelance marketplaces and service communities full of people who want to help—most for a very reasonable price—and some for free!

This book is interactive!
Scan with the Layar App for
updates, bonus material and more

Security Alert: Best Practices for Hiring Help

I've hired plenty of complete strangers to help me with my business, and I have had mostly positive experiences. I attribute my good fortune to both luck and thoughtful hiring. Here are a few things to keep in mind before entrusting people with your projects.

- ✔ Look for providers with a long history of good reviews. Avoid new accounts for projects that might involve sensitive information. Also, make sure you read through the reviews to make sure they're not staged. You can sometimes tell if they're all the same length or style, or if they all comment on the same feature.

- ✔ Secure your passwords as much as you can. Some services, such as MailChimp (Page 144) and WordPress (Page 47), will let you add users with limited privileges. Other times you may want to use a password sharing service such as LastPass (Page 21) that will let you share the information without revealing the actual password.

- ✔ Test the waters before you open all the doors. If you're looking for regular help with a password-protected site or other vulnerable project, start with a smaller task that involves less access instead of the whole project.

Freelancer Marketplaces

Elance

Fiverr

Guru

oDesk

Need to build a new website? Or clean up an old database? Or revamp your marketing material? Help is on the way.

When I need something done, my first thought is always **Fiverr**. Fiverr is a marketplace of literally thousands of people who do all kinds of stuff—for $5.

Five bucks. Yes, indeed.

✔ Create a simple banner ad

✔ Write a customized limerick

✔ Make a tough decision

✔ Tweet your message to thousands of followers

✔ Record a voiceover in a native British accent

✔ Add music to your video

✔ Send your child a personalized letter from Santa Claus

✔ Create a QR Code

And on, and on and on. Hilarious and fun!

The first time I used Fiverr, I spent about $100 trying things out; and I was very pleasantly surprised with the results. I ended up with several videos that range from "eh" to "WOW!" — All for $5!

Since then I've spent hundreds on little projects, everything from a jingle for Your Nerdy Best Friend to promo videos from the Posh English Lady to expertise to fix my WordPress website.

I've had very mixed results with my attempts to get someone to design a T-shirt for me and to design a logo, even though I hired five people at a time in hopes of finding one winner. I also hired several Fiverrs to design cartoon nerds for this book, thinking I'd do a series of original art. I decided to go with a full set I found somewhere else, but some were pretty good, such as this funny little guy.

And I love this version of Your Nerdy Best Friend, packaged and ready to go.

NerdHerd Thumbs Up: Fiverr

Mary Gayle Thomas, CAP-OM, said she learned about Fiverr from yours truly and loves it for "almost anything!" and uses it in conjunction with her role at the International Association of Administrative Professionals.

You can also create more complicated graphics when you purchase multiple gigs, such as this infographic, which I commissioned for $20 plus the cost of the stock image.

Although Fiverr is awesome, you're not always going to get away with a $5 project to advance your business. For larger projects, you can find any number of freelancer marketplaces; and on each site, you can find thousands and thousands of proven experts who can help you with every imaginable task. I think of them as Craigslist on steroids where you can find potential contractors, evaluate their ratings, keep track of their work and control the payment.

When I need to outsource a large project, I head to **Elance**. You describe your project and set the parameters: your budget, your timeline, your hopes and dreams for a successful project. Then you open your project for bids to the marketplace. To find the right person, you might want to search the providers and invite your favorites to bid. If you're commissioning an illustration, for example, hop around in their portfolios to find a designer with a style you like.

You'll probably get from five to 50 proposals; and as they come in, you can add more info to the project description, correspond with the individual bidders, eliminate the yucky ones and rank your top choices. The providers on these sites will have reviews, recommendations and examples—check it all out to make sure you find the right person.

Once you declare a winner on Elance, the site serves as a super-efficient project management tool. You and your new contractor agree on the project terms. On larger projects, you can divide up payments with the milestones. As you work, the system acts like your own Basecamp site (Page 62). Every email you send is cataloged in the system. Every file you exchange is kept in the workroom. Every milestone is tracked. The system even has communication tools such as live chat and screensharing (from join.me, Page 214) built in.

If you were to hire a guy from Craigslist to build your site, you risk freelancer flake out—where the guy gets a girlfriend and has your deposit and you never hear from him again. Elance fights freelancer flake out by holding the funds in escrow—you decide when the work has been done to your satisfaction before you pay the provider. You can find similar protections with **Guru** and **oDesk.**

Extra Hands and Eyes

Fancy Hands	These days I travel to more than 50 speaking engagements every year. I was lugging around a briefcase that was awesome in airport security lanes because all I had to do was unzip it rather than pull out the computer. But the dang thing weighed about 90 pounds, or so it seemed when I slung it over my shoulder trip after trip.
Gigwalk	
TaskRabbit	
WeGoLook	
Zaarly	

To save my shoulders, I had to find a replacement—an attractive, airport-friendly, professional bag with wheels—in a nerd-friendly color! Every time I picked up my old briefcase to travel, I thought about the elusive bag. I would search sometimes, but it was just taking too long to find the perfect one. So I went on abusing my back with the old bag for months.

Then I discovered **Fancy Hands,** a completely nifty site that takes tiny tasks off your plate for $5/request or less. One of the first tasks I sent it was to find me the perfect bag; and within three days, I had a link to an orange, checkpoint-friendly, wheeled tote—on sale even. I was so pleased that I upgraded to 25 tasks a month for $65, and it helps me set appointments, track down lost mail, create cool graphics, research tech tools—you name it—all kinds of little 15-minute tasks that can take me out of work mode and make me lose more time.

Gigwalk, TaskRabbit, WeGoLook and **Zaarly** are similar marketplaces where people who have time to help are on call for people who need help. The struggling economy is fueling these sites as people abandon the traditional workforce and start their own small businesses.

Crowdsourced Design Marketplaces

99designs

crowdSPRING

LogoMyWay

Let's say your organization has a big event every year, and you're looking for a logo that would brand the conference series. You could hire your favorite graphic designer to come up with 10 to 20 ideas for several hundred to several thousand dollars. Or you could hold a logo design contest on a crowdsourcing site for $200+ to have dozens of designers come up with ideas that you could narrow down to your top choices and share with your potential attendees for a vote.

I adore these kinds of contests, both for finding the perfect logo and for strengthening your community. Rather than getting one expert's ideas for your logo, you get ideas from many. And as the contest continues, you can give feedback to your top contenders to get them to refine and rework the colors and designs to help bring your vision to life. The first time I used **LogoMyWay,** I narrowed my logo to four favorites, then I let my newsletter subscribers vote—more than 250 people expressed their opinions, and many were very excited and involved.

But many in the professional design community hate them. I once received a very long, very thorough "shame on you" email from a designer friend. Sites like these, she said, devalue the work that a designer does. They are rife with copyright infringement issues. They exploit talented design artists. And they don't produce quality, well-thought-out work.

I've used LogoMyWay twice, and I enjoyed the process each time. The site claims that the community self-polices, thus ensuring that designers who steal from others are rapidly kicked off. Is my Nerdy Best Friend logo an award winner? Probably not. But am I proud to display it on my stuff? You bet!

On these sites, you can kick off a logo or other design contest with a $200+ contest award offer. There are always extra little costs, like a "featured contest" fee and the site's commission. I'd recommend bumping your contest up at least $100 over the minimum to attract the maximum number of entries. But even with the little extras, you'll probably end up paying less than with a private design company; and you may have more fun in the process. Both **99designs** and **crowdSPRING** offer even more types of design contests, from book covers to T-shirt designs to websites.

Crowdsourced Funding

	You may have heard of **Kickstarter**—it's arguably
Indiegogo	the most well-known of the new sites that help you
Kickstarter	raise money from friends, family and strangers.

Indiegogo may be No. 2 in the market, but it's hard to tell because crowdsourced funding sites are quite the rage.

On most of these sites, you set up your project along with levels of sponsorship. For example, if you're looking to make a nerdy widget that will cost $50, you set up a sponsorship level of maybe $40 to get one widget hot off the assembly line; a $100 sponsorship gets three widgets plus a signed picture of the widget staff; and for $1,000, you'll send 25 widgets and fly out to give the sponsor a kiss. Once your site is live, you send it to everyone you know and try to generate even more buzz to reach the fundraising goal you set for the project.

Kickstarter focuses on creative projects and a stringent review process (see Behind the Glasses: My Kickstarter Story, Page 256), and you have to achieve your fundraising goal before you get any money. Indiegogo lets anyone with an idea start a campaign, and you can sign up for Flexible Funding, which still allows you to get the money you collected even if you don't reach your goal. These two sites are free to set up your project, but you'll pay 7 percent to 12 percent in commission plus credit card processing fees.

Outside Help at a Glance
(recommended tools in **bold**)

99designs	Crowdsourced graphic designs plus ready-made logo catalog	Stock logos for $99, or design contests starting at $149	99designs.com
crowdSPRING	43 categories of crowdsourced contests including logo design, company naming and writing projects	Projects start at $269	crowdspring.com
Elance	**Freelancer database for every item on your to-do list**	**Per-project or hourly pricing**	**elance.com**
Fancy Hands	**Virtual assistants for small tasks starting at $5/request**	**Monthly subscriptions start at 5 requests per month for $25**	**fancyhands.com**
Fiverr	**Community of freelancers who will do anything for $5**	**Ummm, five bucks!**	**fiverr.com**
Gigwalk	Freelance marketplace of surveyors, secret shoppers and location researchers via iOS app	Average gig payment is $10-$15/job	gigwalk.com
Guru	Freelancer database with advanced tools to help you filter candidates to find the best provider	Per-project or hourly pricing	guru.com
Indiegogo	Crowdsourced funding site with no project limitations or application process	7%-12% of money raised goes to fees	indiegogo.com
Kickstarter	The original crowdsourced funding site for creative projects	8%-10% of money collected goes to fees	kickstarter.com
LogoMyWay	**Crowdsourced logo designs plus ready-made logo catalog**	**Contests are minimum $200 plus 10% fee, or $295 for ready-made logos**	**logomyway.com**

254

Outside Help at a Glance (continued)

oDesk	Freelance marketplace plus design contests	Per-project or hourly pricing	odesk.com
TaskRabbit	Database of background-checked freelancers to help with everything from closet organization to dataentry to IKEA assembly	Set the price, and lowest bid from freelancers gets the job	taskrabbit.com
WeGoLook	Nationwide database of inspectors who check out items you want to purchase or verify	Inspection reports start at $59	wegolook.com
Zaarly	Community of service providers from cupcake bakers to party planning to rides to the airport	Varies from a few bucks to thousands	zaarly.com

Online Education

Coursera

edX

Khan Academy

Skillshare

Udacity

Udutu

Imagine yourself telling your colleagues, "I'm taking a course on human-computer interaction at Stanford in the fall." You'd sound super cool and extra smart, and the fact that the course was free and open to all could be your little secret. Or perhaps you could casually mention that *you* have an online university yourself—a set of courses you've developed to help others.

The World Wide Web has made it possible for you to learn and teach online, for little or no money.

I'm really impressed with the vast amount of free education available to all, most notably these days the many universities that offer free online courses and education. **Coursera** has the most robust catalog by far, with offerings from 33 universities, including Stanford, Princeton, Brown and all kinds of other institutions your mother would love to say you attended. **EdX** has courses from Harvard, MIT and Berkeley, among many others.

Behind the Glasses: My Kickstarter Story

When I started working on this book, I received word that the publisher of my first book had gone out of business! Don't you hate it when that happens?

Rather than search for another publisher, I decided to take this project on myself—with the help of a few nerdy friends. It took me about two weeks to put together a proposal for Kickstarter to raise money to produce the book, but to my surprise it rejected me right away, citing its policy to support creative works, not nonfiction self-help books. After I got over the sting of being labeled not creative enough, I decided to run my own crowdsourced funding project on my site.

I set up the payments through PayPal, and I ended up generating almost $4,000 with the help of almost 60 supporters, the people I affectionately call the NerdHerd (see the list on Page V). NerdHerd members helped me pick the cover and received special bonus material and an exclusive webinar, in addition to their signed copies of the book.

The formats vary, but many of them include video lectures with online discussion forums and regular assignments. At the end, you receive certificates of completion or the like. Sites such as **Udacity** are even starting to offer college credit or even an entire degree (for a price), such as the Georgia Tech master's degree in computer science, which will start accepting students in the fall of 2014.

The **Khan Academy's** founder's niece needed some help in math, so he started using online tools to tutor her. Then he graduated to YouTube videos, which became so popular that he quit his job to found the Khan Academy to offer education to all. It has 3,400+ educational videos; and you can watch, test yourself and keep track of your coursework. The site is perfect for anyone from school kids to seasoned professionals.

Skillshare is another general education site, but this time you're learning from seasoned professionals. It offers both online and in-person classes, with prices starting at around $15. And if you have something to teach, **Udutu** lets you create and share coursework to create your own online university. The course authoring tool is free, and hosting is $19 a month—great for associations looking to create custom courses for their industries, plus small businesses wanting to create a training system for their products or establish their expertise.

NerdHerd Favorite: Bookboon

NerdHerd member Nancy McCulley (Your80-20Assistant.com) loves **Bookboon,** a free resource for online business and travel books and textbooks.

Online Education at a Glance

(recommended tools in **bold**)

Bookboon	Downloadable textbooks, business books and travel guides	Free	bookboon.com
Coursera	Free courses from 33 universities, including Stanford, Princeton and Brown	Free	coursera.org
edX	Free courses from Harvard, MIT and Berkeley	Free	edx.org
Khan Academy	Renowned mini-course site for kids through adults	Free	khanacademy.org
Skillshare	Marketplace of education from professionals, from cooking and crafts to how to fund your startup	Starting at $15	skillshare.com
Udacity	Free college-level courses	Free	udacity.com
Udutu	**Course creation site**	**Free to create course, and optional hosting is $19/month**	**udutu.com**

Subject Index

Subject Index

This book is interactive!
Scan with the Layar App for
updates, bonus material and more

Tool Index

Tool Index

Tool Index

Tool Index

Y

Z

About Your Nerdy Best Friend

Beth Ziesenis

Author. Speaker. Nerd.

BETH ZIESENIS, aka Your Nerdy Best Friend, nerds for a living. A longtime technology enthusiast, Beth scours the internet for free and bargain tech tools and apps that help anyone who uses computers or mobile devices.

A MeetingsNet Editors' Pick for Favorite Speaker of 2013, Beth shares her favorite tech tools to thousands of event attendees every year, as well as online at YourNerdyBestFriend.com.

Beth lives in beautiful San Diego with her triathlete husband, D.J. Rausa, and their lazy cat, Mickey Mouse. She spends her non-nerdy time running marathons with The Leukemia & Lymphoma Society, where Beth and D.J. have together raised more than $25,000 in the fight against cancer. The cat has been no help.

Made in the USA
San Bernardino, CA
15 November 2014